D0855837

GEOFFREY BOCCA

Prentice-Hall, Inc., Englewood Cliffs, New Jersey 07632

Library of Congress Cataloging in Publication Data

Bocca, Geoffrey.
You can write a novel.

"A Spectrum Book."
Includes index.
1. Fiction—Authorship. I. Title.
PN3365.B57 1983 808.3 83-13990
ISBN 0-13-976845-9
ISBN 0-13-976837-8 (pbk.)

A Spectrum Book. Printed in the United States of America.

1 2 3 4 5 6 7 8 9 10

ISBN 0-13-976845-9

ISBN 0-13-976837-8 {PBK.}

Editorial/production supervision by Betsy Torjussen
Cover design by Ben Santora
Manufacturing buyer: Pat Mahoney

This book is available at a special discount when ordered in bulk quantities. Contact Prentice-Hall, Inc., General Publishing Division, Special Sales, Englewood Cliffs, N.J. 07632.

Prentice-Hall International, Inc., *London*
Prentice-Hall of Australia Pty. Limited, *Sydney*
Prentice-Hall Canada Inc., *Toronto*
Prentice-Hall of India Private Limited, *New Delhi*
Prentice-Hall of Japan, Inc., *Tokyo*
Prentice-Hall of Southeast Asia Pte. Ltd., *Singapore*
Whitehall Books Limited, *Wellington, New Zealand*
Editora Prentice-Hall do Brasil Ltda., *Rio de Janeiro*

CONTENTS

Dedicated to Dr. Clifton Lanier Warren
chairman of the Department of Creative Studies
Central State University, Edmund, Oklahoma

ACKNOWLEDGMENTS

Grateful acknowledgment is given to the following for granting permission to reprint passages from their publications:

The quotation on pages 82–84 from *Ulysses*, by James Joyce, copyright © 1914, 1918 by Margaret Caroline Anderson and renewed 1942, 1946 by Nora Joseph Joyce, is reprinted by permission of Random House, Inc. and The Bodley Head.

The excerpt on pages 90–91 from *Amanda in Spain*, by Geoffrey Bocca, copyright © 1975 by Geoffrey Bocca, is reprinted by permission of Zebra Books.

The excerpt on pages 93–94 from *Lolita*, by Vladimir Nabokov, copyright © 1955 by Vladimir Nabokov, is reprinted by permission of Mrs. Vladimir Nabokov and G. P. Putnam's Sons.

The quotation on page 101 from *Aimez Vous Brahms*, by Françoise Sagan, copyright © 1960 by John Murray, Ltd., is reprinted by permission of the publishers, E. P. Dutton, Inc., and John Murray, Ltd.

The excerpt on pages 101–102 from *Scruples*, by Judith Krantz, copyright © 1978 by Steve Krantz Productions, is reprinted by permission of Crown Publishers, Inc.

The quotation on pages 115–116 from *How Right You Are, Jeeves*, by P. G. Wodehouse, copyright © 1960 by P. G. Wodehouse, is reprinted by permission of Simon & Schuster, Inc., the author, and the author's agents, Scott Meredith Literary Agency, Inc., 845 Third Avenue, New York, New York 10022.

INTRODUCTION

I was forty years old when I published my first novel.

I had already published perhaps ten or eleven nonfiction books, including three that had reached the best-seller list, so I should have been happy continuing to do what apparently came naturally to me. But—like you—I was a frustrated novelist and could not keep my hands off the *genre*. I still have several of my early fiction manuscripts. Re-reading them I don't think they are at all bad, but my agent shot them down and refused even to submit them to publishers. I struggled on.

Over the years, friends of mine—journalists and nonfiction writers like myself—announced that their first novels had been accepted, by Doubleday or Knopf or Harper & Row or André Deutsch, glamorous names like that, and were off to the Greek islands to begin their next. I congratulated them and hoped that the green of my envy did not show too vividly.

After several false starts I wrote a thriller, set against the background of the Berlin Wall, that I thought was pretty good. I delivered it one Friday afternoon to my New York literary agent, who promised to read it over the weekend.

It was not his judgment that surprised me, but the way he delivered it. On Monday we were having a drink together at Toots

Shor's, then on West 51st Street. With us were John D. McDonald, the late Quentin Reynolds, and a few others. We were talking small talk when out of the blue, my agent slapped my back and said, "This guy is one of the best magazine writers in this country. You'd think he'd be happy with that, but oh, my goodness, no. His trouble is he wants to be a novelist. He can't write a novel. He will never be a novelist if he keeps trying for the rest of his life."

McDonald, Reynolds, and the others laughed, and I pretended to laugh too. But inwardly I seethed. It was as if a gauntlet had been thrown down. Until this moment I might actually have accepted the idea that I couldn't write fiction. But not now! Next time they could join *me* in laughing.

That night I sat down to write a new novel. When it was finished I showed it to Knox Burger, then senior editor at Gold Medal Books and today a distinguished agent in his own right. His verdict: "It needs a lot of work, and anyway, the time isn't ripe for that kind of satirical novel."

I wasn't beaten but I needed a breather, so I went back to working on a true-crime book, *The Life and Death of Sir Harry Oakes*. About six months later I saw Knox Burger again, this time in the old Absinthe House on West 48th Street. "That novel of yours," he said. "What happened to it?"

"Nothing."

"I'd like to show it to somebody."

I was stunned. This was the first time I had ever received anything other than flat rejection. I found the manuscript on a shelf, blew the dust off it, and left it at Burger's reception desk. A month later, my agent said to me curiously, "I've just had a telephone call. Do you know anything about a novel called *Commander Amanda*? I've received an offer for it."

And that's how my first novel, *Commander Amanda*, a spoof set in occupied France during World War II, was sold. It was subsequently translated into German, French, Dutch, Swedish, Hebrew, Spanish, Portuguese, Greek, Finnish, Japanese, and a few other languages. It was to be the first of five novels I would write about the same heroine, Amanda Nightingale (the others being *Resort to War, Amanda's Castle, Amanda in Spain*, and *Amanda in Berlin*), and, along the way, I have published six or seven other novels under various names. I have shelved my newest novel just long enough to write this book.

It can be argued, and I have argued it myself, that I have not done a lick of work in the last thirty years. The reasons for that are simple: I love writing and I write easily. But useful though they are, neither of these attributes has anything to do with *good* writing. Indeed, many of the world's greatest writers—Joseph Conrad and Graham Greene, to name just two—have found writing an agony.

You can divide writers into four interwoven categories, *facile* (not in any pejorative sense), *agonized*, *disciplined*, and *undisciplined*. Thus, Greene and Conrad are agonized and disciplined. Tolstoy is agonized and undisciplined. Charles Dickens is facile and undisciplined, as is James Michener; whereas Saul Bellow is facile and disciplined. I hope you find it as consoling as I do to think that people of such diverse temperaments could all be fine writers.

When I first came to America from England as a young Fleet Street newspaperman seeking wider expression, I was granted an interview with Mr. Sumner Blossom, editor of *American Monthly* magazine and the doyen of American magazine editors. "So, young fella," he said. "You want to be a real writer? I have only one piece of advice for you."

I poised my pencil over my pad.

"You don't need to write this down. I'll tell you: Don't talk to anybody about what you are writing."

He called that *advice*! His only advice! He saw that I looked disconcerted and deeply chagrined. He said, "I'm not for one moment suggesting that people would steal your ideas. You are more likely to bore them than intrigue them. No, what happens is this: you have an idea that fills you with enthusiasm. You want to tell people about your great idea. And maybe you do have the best idea in the world. But tell it to eight friends and you will have lost all interest in writing it. The impetus, the momentum that should have gone on to your typewriter or your stenopad or your tape-machine, has disappeared into thin air, into and out of the ears of strangers who have nothing to do with either your idea or your destiny."

I now believe this is nearly the best literary advice I ever received. It has become a part of me. Today I am *incapable* of discussing what I am writing, even with my publishers. A novel must be wrapped in silence.

And publishers understand. Publishers have a pleasant tradition of taking writers to lunch from time to time. Without exception they will ask one of two questions. The first is: "How's the book coming along?"

If the reply is "fine," that's the end of the business conversation, and the rest of the meal is devoted to malicious gossip about mutual friends. If the reply is "I am having trouble" or "I am having a block," the publisher's filet of sole will pause on its fork in midair and the question will be, "Is there anything we can do to help at this end?"

Invariably the reply to that is "No, thank you," and that will be that.

So, by all means tell your friends and loved ones that you are writing a novel—but nothing more. If it is humanly possible, don't even talk about it to your husband or your wife. Write it first. Talk when it is finished.

That is not to say you won't ever need help. You can tell that from the fact that so many books are dedicated to their authors' editors. What that means is that the writer has sat looking at an empty page for hour after hour until the editor has tossed in a suggestion or two that succeeded in breaking the creative logjam. The dependence of Hemingway, Scott Fitzgerald, and Faulkner on the wisdom of Maxwell Perkins of Scribner's is famous. But the fact remains that the actual writing of a novel is a solitary business—one that benefits from being shared with others only on rare and special occasions.

For years I fretted at the selfishness of my profession. Writers sit at their desks, keeping their secrets, the tricks of their trade, their techniques, their priorities. As artists, they are at the opposite end of the spectrum from actors who have to give their all night after night. Writers keep everything. They squirrel away their work and their knowledge. They hand in a finger-stained, wine-daubed, criss-crossed manuscript and get back a beautiful object—their own book.

Because I felt I wanted to convey to potential authors something of what I knew, I laid out feelers with the admirable organization the Associated Writing Program (A.W.P.), which has headquarters at Old Dominion University, Norfolk, Virginia. There I was put, by Gale Arnoux, in touch with several institutions. One or two were fashionable Eastern colleges that did not attract me. I was afraid of being overwhelmed by dilletantism, Gucci loafers, and designer jeans. I wanted serious post-graduate students, with a novel or more in them, who seriously wanted professional help. So when the offer came from Central State University in Edmond, Oklahoma, I thought it might be just what I was looking for, and I was right.

I hope that I helped my students, several of whom have gone on to see their work published. In any case, I certainly learned a surprising amount about myself as a technician.

Dr. Clifton Warren, chairman of Creative Writing at C.S.U., would say to me in exasperation, part mock, part serious, "The trouble with you is that you are an instinctive writer. You know nothing about plot, dialogue, narrative, characterization. You just know what is wrong and what is right. When you go wrong, you know it and put it right."

I am afraid he had a point, and that point bears on how this book is written. I will not fall back on standard, stereotyped mathematical formulas for the creation of a novel. I couldn't if I tried. I have listened, astonished and frequently dismayed, when I visited other universities. I have watched intelligent students writing notes, recording observations from their professor on such esoteric matters as when to introduce the third character, how the second chapter should contrast with the first, how the baddie should contrast with the goodie, the necessary length of a novel, and the length of each chapter. Invariably their professors were quoting from other manuals. I have tried to read the other manuals myself but usually couldn't understand them.

Mind you, I don't disdain the purely academic approach to writing. It's just that there's no substitute for *doing*. Or for experience of life. In my time I have been a newspaper reporter, a sailor, a soldier, and briefly in the theater. All were invaluable in the study of human nature and human beings. To the novelist nobody is a bore. (Including bores. Some of the greatest characters in fiction are bores—Dr. Pangloss in *Candide*, Pierre in *War and Peace*, Tesman in *Hedda Gabler.* Fascinating bores pour out of the pages of Charles Dickens. I should even go so far as to say that most of Graham Greene's characters are bores.)

At a cocktail party in Washington, D.C., I recently heard someone—a sociologist, more likely than not—cornering a victim and saying something like, "Don't you believe that in order to perceive the whole, you must recreate the various elements of human experience to assure the necessary balance between what is concept and what is defined knowledge?"

I reached for ballpoint and paper and scribbled desperately to record this gorgeous gibberish. Never mind the poor victim in the corner. I wanted to get the gobbledygook on paper for some future character in some future book. The fact that it was so meaningless and pretentious was what gave it its value to a novelist. It could illuminate a character better than a page of description.

For the novelist, nothing in human experience is lost. As a novelist I have to regard those people who walk the streets with earphones over their ears with pity. These zombies have removed themselves from the fascinating details of the world around them—which is the stuff from which all novels and, indeed, all art are created.

Goethe said that he wished he could write in any language but German. I doubt that he would ever have said that if his native language had been English. I firmly believe that our polyglot language—with its vast borrowings from the Anglo-Saxon, French, German, Latin, and a dozen other tongues—is the richest, subtlest, and most beautiful in the world. It's an incredible gift to the English-speaking novelist.

If you want an indication of how powerful our "mongrel" language is, just consider how much trouble the Germans, the French, and even the Russians are now having trying to protect their languages against the encroachments of English. (The French call it *franglais*. Some time ago in Paris I passed a new high-rise cooperative apartment building that advertised itself as "*Des buildings de grand standing.*") And the most precious possessions any young Muscovite can treasure are *koboi blujins*. Oscar Wilde, Irishman, said, "The English took our language away, which left us with no alternative but to perfect theirs." How lucky he was! But then Oscar probably never doubted it for a moment.

All creative art is magic, an evocation of the unsuspected, unknown, unseen into persuasive and believable forms. Readers have to believe what you are saying, no matter how wild the theme. They want something new in each succeeding sentence, never to feel replete until they come to the end. In the same way, the writing of a novel is a constant renewal of oneself, as a writer and as a person.

Many people—students, interviewers, and others—have asked me, "What do you consider the best book you have written?" I hate that question, because my answer is so corny it makes me feel and sound like a fathead. My answer is: "The book I am writing now." And that is because I keep hoping that the best sentence I will ever write will be the next sentence I put on paper. If I ever hoped otherwise, I would take another job.

1

GETTING STARTED

Everyone has his own method of writing. Ernest Hemingway typed standing up. Edgar Wallace dictated his novels from midnight to morning into an early form of dictaphone. Richard Condon uses every new gadget that comes on the market and currently declares that his life has been revolutionized by a word processor. I can think of a score of writers who can write only in longhand. I, on the other hand, am so conditioned to composing on a typewriter that I even type my checks. If the KGB arrested me and sought to break me, they would have only to take away my typewriter, for I should then be like a chain-smoker without cigarettes.

Far more important than the ways writers get their ideas onto paper are the intellectual and physical resources with which they surround themselves. All writers pride themselves on their reference libraries, but there are a few basic books without which it would scarcely be possible to write any novel. One is a good dictionary. I use two: the *American Heritage Dictionary* and *Webster's New Collegiate Dictionary*, but there are several others as good or better.

All but indispensable is *Roget's Thesaurus*. If you are sick of using the word *terrific*, Roget will suggest *famous*, *great*, *glorious*, *dazzling, splendid, magnificent, marvelous, wonderful, superb.* Even if you thought that your original word was the only one that could express what you wanted to say, *Roget's Thesaurus* will usually give you all the alternatives you need. Some years ago the New York agent James Street went into the hospital for a stomach ailment, the result of wounds sustained in World War II. His stay was either shortened or lengthened by a limerick sent to him by a colleague, the late John Starr:

That amiable agent, Jim Street,
Performed a most whimsical feat.
He stuffed his pilorus
With *Roget's Thesaurus*,
For he thought they were words he should eat.

I get a lot of help from two dictionaries of quotations, the two-volume *Shorter Oxford English Dictionary* and *Bartlett's Familiar Quotations.* The former is English, the latter American. Frequently I find in one what I have sought in vain from the other.

If possible, you should have *The Oxford Universal Dictionary,* either in its thirteen-volume edition or in the small-type two-volume set that comes with a magnifying glass. I don't. I need it rarely, but when I need it, I need it badly. Probably you, as I, have friends who own one. And nothing delights a friend more than to be asked for a reference.

The complete *Oxford* lists not only every word, but also the first recorded use of that word in the English language. For example, recently I needed to discover the origin of the word "brunch." I assumed it to be an American word, since the English tradition of spending midday to 2:00 P.M. in the local pub makes the American brunch tradition almost impossible. I learned from the *Oxford* that the first known use of the word appeared in England in *Punch* magazine in 1897: "It is considered fashionable nowadays to 'brunch.'"

Besides a dictionary, a good atlas is essential, and so are a

British *Who's Who* and a *Who's Who in America*, which contains all sorts of references to colleges, titles, addresses, awards, degrees, and so on. Also, I am still surprised by how often I turn to *Dictionary of Foreign Terms in the English Language*, compiled by David Carroll and published by Hawthorn. It is useful if you have a character who is a lawyer or an academic or merely pretentious.

Many people swear by *Fowler's Modern English Usage* and others by Strunk and White's *Elements of Style*. Both are fine books, but for some reason I seldom consult either.

Not all of the books in a novelist's basic reference library have to do with words and language. I don't think I have ever written a novel without referring to the *Dictionary of Design and Decoration*, a big coffee-table book published by Viking. That book—or any other illustrated dictionary of design—is an invaluable aid for describing a style, period, house, or room.

A good fat illustrated book about Hollywood and the movies has many uses. Among other things, it helps if you seek a precise photographic image of one of your characters. Since a movie contract lurks in the minds of all of us (and also in the minds of our publishers), it does no harm to have a particular actor in mind when creating a character. This doesn't result in stereotyping, for as the character develops, he or she will develop an independent personality. I always thought of the central character of my novel *The Fourth Horseman* to be a kind of Michael Caine person, but my publisher saw him as Sean Connery. Since the book was never made into a movie, it didn't matter.

The point is that it is extraordinarily useful to be able to visualize your characters precisely. The jowls of Wallace Beery, the radiance of Norma Shearer, the straight nose of Robert Taylor, the nitwit expression on the face of Una Merkel, Brian Donlevy's sneer—all may fit one of your characters and help both your descriptions and even your understanding of how the characters may react to certain situations.

Other essential reference books will relate to the specific subject matter or setting of your novel—books about cars or guns or Regency costumes or life in Nelson's navy or voodoo rituals—the list of categories is endless. Such reference collections have to be assembled for each particular novel that you write. They need not be exhaustive, just good enough to keep you from making unnecessary mistakes.

Once you've gotten your reference books in order, prepare your desk: plenty of No. 2 pencils (manuscripts should always be corrected with erasable pencils), stapler, staple-remover, white correction tape to erase typing errors, and correction fluid for more prolonged errors.

Incidentally, if you travel abroad, a word concerning correction tape. Once when I was returning to the United States from Quito, Ecuador, I was ordered by the customs officer to open my typewriter. The fundament of any erasing paper is chalk, which whitens out the error. But the sediment left in the case of my overused portable typewriter looked suspiciously like heroin! I am happy to say that innocence won out in the end, but as Wellington said of Waterloo, it was a close-run thing.

Now you should plan, or rather not plan, your office. Most writers' offices are congeries of calculated clutter. In all the homes I have had—in London, New York, Hollywood, the French Riviera, Ibiza—I have always chosen the smallest and most insignificant room in which to work: a room without distractions. Instead of looking at paintings or wall hangings, many writers look up from their typewriters to study some slogan or piece of self-advice that they have affixed to their walls as part of their personal disciplines. Harold Robbins keeps a list of the birth dates of his characters. The late Catherine Drinker Bowen, distinguished biographer of John Adams and others, kept a sign "Will the reader turn the page?" Ian Fleming used to keep a sign reading, "Stop smoking, you gutless swine!"

Mine is a World War II poster that I bought at the Imperial War Museum in London. It shows a provocative girl with ambiguous lynxlike eyes, wearing a see-through dress. She is surrounded by three admiring officers of the Army, Royal Navy, and Royal Air Force, holding drinks in their hands. The caption reads, "Keep mum; she's not so dumb. Careless talk costs lives." Exactly what this conveys to me I cannot say, but it seems to help.

When Somerset Maugham moved into the Villa Mauresque, his mansion in the south of France, he surveyed the masterpiece of interior decoration that he had ordered. His office looked out over his swimming pool and a stupendous view of the Mediterranean, with the promontory of Monte Carlo on his left and Cap Ferrat on his right.

To the designer he said, "I want only one change made. Turn my desk so that it faces the wall."

Now you are almost ready. You know the novel you want to write, you have organized your library, and you have made your physical preparations. Now you must submit to a crucial bit of discipline: You must determine your audience. You must understand your readers at least as well as you understand the characters in your book, for indeed they *will be* characters in your book—the most important ones of all. If there is a general rule about addressing an audience it is this: Aim high rather than low. Readers may forgive you for going over their heads occasionally, but never for insulting their intelligence.

I see my audience as predominantly female, because my fan mail is mostly from women. I see her as a graduate student who has read Dickens and Shakespeare. She is a perfectionist who will not be fooled by humbug. She demands a lot of me, but if I set my sights any lower I would not only lose her as a reader, but lose most of the pleasure I get from writing at all.

Determining your audience is, of course, only part of the psychological preparation you need to bring to the writing of a novel. One of my favorite *New Yorker* cartoons shows a businessman father in a deckchair, pad on knee, staring out over the water. At his side stands his son, plaintively holding a broken toy. The caption is, "Not now, son. Dad is composing an interoffice memorandum."

I suspect I like this cartoon for reasons other than those the cartoonist had in mind. I sympathize with the man in the cartoon completely. An interoffice memorandum needs words. It needs to be well written. Like a novel or a short story or a poem, it must convey information *and* produce a calculated effect. To write a good interoffice memorandum implies not merely verbal skill but an entire frame of mind. Think of the psychological attributes that the memorandist, or any writer, must bring to the enterprise of writing.

The first is *professional curiosity*, the acquired art of making a mental note, even subconsciously, of what other people take for granted or don't notice. For the novelist it may be the chewed fingernails on an otherwise well-groomed woman (why is she so nervous?) or the Brigade of Guards tie on the bum who asks you for a quarter. Will a Canadian dime fit a United States telephone? Why is a solitary light shining in an office building at midnight? What will be the future of the student on the campus, her textbooks clutched to her bosom? what textbooks? does she smoke? is she worried about her credits? should she lose weight? As a novelist you are intrigued by every detail.

The next is *professional discipline*. This consists of sitting down to work without interruption and not leaving your desk until you have achieved the goal you have set for yourself for that day. Anyone who sets work aside and waits for the Muse to strike will wait forever. The Muse proves more and more elusive the longer you await it, but it is remarkably available if you go to seek it every day and grab it by the throat.

Next, *patience*. Writing is a slow, time-consuming business, and this is especially true of novel writing. The process seems endless, and the more you rewrite, the more rewriting seems to be necessary. It is like Alice among the bulrushes. No matter how many she gathers, more beautiful blooms appear just beyond her reach. Once submitted, you might have to wait three months, four months, five months, or longer while it sits in the publisher's office. Then, once accepted, allow eight months to a year before you finally get your author's copies. Face the depressing fact that when the novel you are writing finally hits the bookstores, you will be at least two years older than you are now.

I have only a few firm rules, but the following is one of the more important. As soon as my manuscript has gone off to the publisher, I begin a new book. Even before the manuscript is finished, thoughts about the new book are floating about in my mind, and notes are accumulating in a new file. That way I am so high on the book I am about to begin that the previous book has become almost a thing of the past. I hardly think about it. Good reviews, bad reviews have almost no relevance for me. All that matters is what I am writing *today.* Never wait for the mailman to knock. Never wait to see what the critics have to say. Never wait for the sales returns. When the bell tolls, it will toll.

For the next attribute I can think of no other word but *squirreling*. An author is a sort of intellectual squirrel. He tears things out of newspapers that interest him. He collects words and thoughts. A novelist rarely even respects books. He tends to tear out and file sequences that he thinks will advance his own thought processes.

Try to remember good snippets of conversation you have heard, and later write them down. The young lady I overheard saying to her friend in the subway yesterday, "The biggest goddamn fool on this planet would never dare mess with a really mad Scorpio" might one day see that line in a future novel of mine. Or more likely she will never know. But write it down *afterwards*, never on the spot. Nothing annoys a person more than to realize that he or she has just said something original and that someone else—especially a professional writer—is going to make personal capital out of it!

The last is *sociability.* I believe that a writer must meet as many people as he can. Everyone is a potential reader whose interests and requirements must be understood, and for the novelist, almost everyone could be material for his novel. I cannot count the number of friends and colleagues who elected to escape the rat race of New York and London and go someplace quiet to write that Great Novel. New Yorkers usually move to the woods and streams of New England, buy a property overlooking a lake, and imagine they are Thoreau. Londoners move to the south of France or Majorca or Ibiza. What most of them have in common is that they are never heard of again.

I suppose I could go on enumerating preliminaries for many more pages, but, finally, writing is a matter of doing. So let us assume that you have made all the necessary psychological, intellectual, and physical preparations and are now ready to begin the real work of putting words on paper. What are some of the technical aspects you should bear in mind? That is what the remainder of this book will be about.

I should warn you that I do not intend to carve up the subject of novel writing into discrete packages, each with neat little labels such as *characterization*, *style*, *plot*, *setting*, and so on, because it is false to imagine that these elements can really be separated from one another. I shall treat them simply as they arise in the natural course of the discussion.

2

RULES OF THE GAME

I heard John le Carré say on television some time ago that he cannot remember the actual physical work of writing any of his novels. His memory is a blank. I checked my own experience and realized to my surprise that my experience was the same. My nonfiction books I can recall precisely, but I have to check back to the flyleaves of my various novels to remember even *when* I wrote them. They are as hard to recall as the pangs of childbirth (at least so I am assured by persons of the appropriate sex).

You are writing your novel. In every other way you are an ordinary person. You eat, drink, sleep, pay your bills, go to the movies. But in fact you are living in a void that you are gradually filling up with your story, your narrative, your characters, your constant changes of ideas, your ever-renewing sources of inspiration. Only when the void is filled and the novel finished are you back in the world again. Those around you may see no difference in you. But *you* know. You have returned. Your trip around the moon and over the rainbow is over. No more will you wake up in the middle of the night with a flash of inspiration to be jotted down before it goes forever back into the unconscious. You are just an ordinary person again.

What exactly were you doing while you were away in that

other world of the imagination? Apart from the fact that you were having fun, you were also doing a lot of hard disciplined work; and you were, to the best of your ability, obeying the iron rules of your craft.

Rules such as what? There are a number of them. But there is one that is so much more important than any of the others that it must have pride of place. It's simply this: *Dramatize, dramatize, dramatize.*

The art of dramatizing begins with characterization. Bring all of your characters to life. You can create a character who is a bore, but you must not make him boring. You can create a rogue, but remember that no man is a rogue to himself. He has his point of view too. ("'I, a crab!' cried the crustacean. 'No, by God, not I! I am myself, myself alone!'") You can go on to create the most beautiful girl in the world, but I will wager all Lombard Street to a china orange that she goes every week to an analyst. You can create a tycoon of limitless wealth, but such tycoons live in fear, more fear than ordinary people can conceive. They fear their friends. They fear their enemies. They fear their children. They fear for their money.

You can create a handsome young man who keeps a yacht in the Cannes Marina, surrounded by gorgeous topless girls, the object of envy, but he is in fact the season's sucker and will end the year in prison in Grasse with no one to visit him at all, except his consul with a food parcel.

The permutations on character are limitless, but it is the wart on the nose that fascinates. Ian Fleming always gave his female characters imperfections: Tiffany Case, to quote just one example, walked with a slight limp. Jake Barnes in *The Sun Also Rises* had been wounded in the most unfortunate place a man can think of.

In the course of a recent summer I met a charming young woman whose arms, I noticed, were freckled to the shoulders. Somehow in the novel I am now writing, my heroine has arms freckled to the shoulders. She is an amalgam of several women I have met. She has a small bosom and wears a T-shirt stating "Flat Girls Feel Good."

Consider giving your central female character a weight problem. Make her a chocaholic. Consider making your male character rather small, or giving him a slight touch of arthritis or gout. Consider anything, but *make your characters human.* If they aren't, no other dramatic devices of plot or style that you may use will ever get off the ground.

You can tell when your characters are adequately human: They become hard to manage. Suppose you have just about finished your novel. You are on your way down the final stretch and your heels have sprouted the wings of Mercury. You write:

> A blood-orange sun was setting behind the Arc de Triomphe, mercifully hiding the monstrous edifice of La Défense on the other side. The first breeezes of winter announced themselves by sidling down the Champs Elysées. Klaxons sounded around the Etoile as if the drivers had never been in a traffic jam before. Andrew sat at the bar of Fouquet's and sipped his vermouth cassis and smiled. He loved Paris at this time of the evening at this season of the year....

"Sorry for intruding..."

You jump in your chair. You thought you were alone. "I beg your pardon! I am working."

"I apologize. I was only trying to help."

"Who are you?"

"I am Andrew, the figment of your imagination."

"Well, buzz off, Andrew. Can't you see I am busy immortalizing you?"

"But the trouble is I don't ... never did...."

"Did what?"

"Love Paris at this time of the evening, or at any season of the year for that matter. I hate Paris. I say so on page one hundred and fifty-three."

"I can change your mind. In fact, I did change your mind. This minute."

"You'll be sorry."

"Whose mind is it anyway? You'll be sorrier than I if you try to complicate my novel at this stage."

"OK, don't get your knickers in a twist. But I am going to laugh like a fool when I see the corner you have painted yourself into in the chapter after next."

What all this means is that your characters have taken over and have a life of their own. It is an exciting moment in the development of your novel. They are real people. They are your friends and your enemies. They live in your dreams. Making love, they arouse you physically. In a bad temper, they upset you. When they die, your tears wet the typewriter keys.

But what a lot of hard work you had to do. What world of guile and craft you had to use in order to bring your characters to this state of grace. To begin with you had to wrestle with the language itself. Here are some of the most important rules that govern that particular travail.

George Orwell said: "Never use a long word where a short word will do." If you are a Henry James or a William Faulkner, you may be able to disagree, but in principle Orwell was right.

By the same token, a short sentence is usually preferable to a long sentence, but not to the extent of irritating the reader like a barking dog. A couple of short sentences should be followed by a longer sentence.

Orwell again: "If it is possible to cut out a word, cut it out."

Always use the most active verb form available: "He ran" is nearly always better than "He was running."

Paragraphs tend to speak for themselves. A writer just *knows* when a paragraph logically ends. I prefer long paragraphs to short ones. Short paragraphs in succession spoil my concentration.

You will find that harsh staccato violent words will come into your brain when you write fast-action narrative and nail-biting sequences. Softer, gentler, more languorous words, words with more vowels and fewer consonants will emerge in scenes of tenderness. Tybalt to Romeo before their duel: "Romeo, the hate I bear thee can afford no better term than this, thou art a villain." Romeo to Juliet after their night of love, "Night's candles are burnt out, and jocund day stands tiptoe on the misty mountain tops."

I shall have more to say about style too, but for the moment I turn to another consideration. Some might not think this important enough for lengthy discussion but I do, from occasionally painful experience. It is this: Choose the names of your characters with the kind of care you would choose your spouse. The analogy is not as bizarre as it sounds. Once you have selected the name of a character and you are deep into the book, it has become a kind of marriage. You are committed, and if you realize you have chosen a bad name, you are either stuck with it or you go through the painful process of divorcing it by whitening it out and substituting another name, a process that might have to be repeated through hundreds of pages.

Avoid names ending in *s*—James, Bess, Edwards, and so on. It will not take you many pages of manuscript to see why. You will find yourself entangled in *James's, Bess's, Edwards's.* Ian Fleming created James Bond as a whim, the name of a friend of his in Jamaica, and he regretted it. Fleming in his novels nearly always refers to "Bond." I put myself into double jeopardy in one book by calling one major French character "Georges" and wasted many man-hours and bottles of correction fluid changing his name to "Pierre." If you decide that a name-change is necessary, try to give your new name the same number of letters or less, never more. A longer name won't fit in the empty space!

The letter X in a name gives, to me at least, the connotation of power, usually a sinister power. In my novel *Nadine,* the bad guy was called Max Paringaux, although when I created him my feeling about X was subconscious rather than conscious. In that brilliant Truffaut movie *The Last Metro*, the menace of the pro-Nazi French theater critic was enhanced by his name, Daxiat.

Similarly, the letter Z in a woman's name can connote exoticism and mystery: Zara, Zita, Zena, not to mention Zsa Zsa and Zuleika.

Avoid having two major characters whose names start with the same letter. It can be confusing to the reader. And yet another hint: Marjorie, Patricia, Carolyn, Ann are all admirable names, but not in the same novel. There is a social sameness which blurs the reader's mind. They create no mental image of conflict. Lace such names with harder, more infrequent names—Olga, Karen, Natalie, Yvonne, Theodora, Phoebe, Wanda—the available list is endless. Simply leaf through a dictionary of Greek mythology or Roman history. But avoid the Celts—names like Siobhan and Blodwin can close books.

The problem occurs more rarely with men's names. Even everyday men's names have a greater range and stronger contrast than women's names, and they are more amenable to nicknames: Sandy, Tug, Bucky, Hank.

For a conventional novel of suspense, crime, or adventure, there is nothing wrong with traditional comic-strip practice: monosyllabic first name, bisyllabic second name—Dick Tracy, Rip Kirby, Steve Canyon, Buzz Sawyer.

Study the masters. After Dickens, two of the great masters in the selection of names are Margaret Mitchell and Ian Fleming. Scarlett, Rhett, Melanie, and Ashley cut slashes between each other's characters. No reader ever has to ask himself "which character is which?" Ian Fleming could mugshot a personality in a name: Oddjob, Shatterhand, Jaws, Tiffany Case, Miss Moneypenny. Name-dropping, if you will pardon the expression, may be instinctive rather than cultivated. Not all writers have the gift. Graham Greene, Ernest Hemingway, Scott Fitzgerald have left us very few truly memorable names.

Take regionalism into account in your selection of names. If I encounter a character from Maine or Vermont called Brunelle or Leduc, I would presume if nothing more were said that he was of French-Canadian or Franco-American origin, thus placing him in sharper focus in my mind. In one novel I call a French war hero Schneider, a German name indicating that he came from Alsace or Lorraine. An officer of the French Army bearing a Germanic name would indicate to the informed reader a virulently anti-German character, and therefore one who would fight for De Gaulle's Free French against the Pétainist influences of Vichy.

I would be inclined to give a working-class urban Frenchman a Polish name. For generations, the coal mines of northern France were worked by Poles (among them, Giereck, former Polish Communist head). A Frenchman with an Italian name would be Mediterranean, either Corsican or Marseillais, indicating either a gangster or a policeman. I would be inclined to give an aristocratic German a Hungarian name, indicating vast Central European estates and deer-hunting. A rich Californian called Gomez is almost by definition a Mexican who made good. A character called Nelson-Smith with an English accent turning up in Arkansas is obviously running away from something, and I wouldn't cash his check.

A working-class girl called Marilyn, or a middle-aged woman named Marlene or Lana or Deanna, does not need to have her age spelled out. The reader is quickly aware of the tastes, class, and priorities of her parents at the time she was born.

The wrong name can seriously upset a reader's concentration, not to mention his basic belief in the character. A student of mine, in an excellent novel, created a rich Chicago Episcopalian boy who thumbed his nose at his parents by joining the Communist party. But he insisted on calling the boy Silk, which to most readers would strongly suggest a Jewish name and would thus upset the social equilibrium of the book.

It is often a good idea to keep a list of names on the wall in front of you, or make a note of interesting names that you run across. If your book has many characters, you may even want to include a list in the introduction, a practice of Erle Stanley Gardner in his Perry Mason books, Charles Dickens in *Bleak House*, and other authors.

Here is another rule with which not everyone would agree,

but I consider important: Use plenty of anecdotes, but be extremely wary of humor. A book is an emotional experience for the writer, and that emotion must be conveyed to the reader. I can count on the fingers of one hand the number of successful humorous living novelists. There are Kurt Vonnegut, John Irving, Richard Condon, and . . . and . . .

I speak from personal experience. I have a natural penchant for humorous writing, in short, I find it hard to resist raising a laugh when one seems called for, and successive publishers have been compelled to tone my humor down. Victor Weybright, the publisher, once reminded me, "Evelyn Waugh was not a successful novelist until he was converted to Catholicism and poured his soul into *Brideshead Revisited.* Only then did people really begin to sit up and start reading his earlier humorous works, such as *Vile Bodies* and *Decline and Fall.*

Max Wilkinson, when he was my agent, told me more than once, "Stop being the amused bystander. You must become emotionally involved in your characters."

Indeed, you can run your finger down the list of best-selling novels and see not the whisper of a smile from top to bottom. My most brilliant university student wrote a comic novel about a man who is mysteriously murdered and comes back as a ghost to find out why. I thought it was hilarious, but I was unable to find one New York publisher who was ready to publish it.

Perhaps that is why most funny movies are either original screenplays or come from the stage. Innes Rose, my London agent, told me, "If you must insist on being funny, write a play."

A rule that you will find in many writing textbooks states that you should only write about things you know firsthand. That is *not* one of *my* rules.

The odds are that the novel you are writing *is* based on personal experience. Ernest Hemingway in *Green Hills of Africa* reminded us that both Tolstoy and Stendhal had seen armed combat in war and Flaubert had witnessed a revolution and the horrors of the Paris Commune of 1870 and that Dostoevsky had been exiled to Siberia. Hemingway wrote the book too early to be able to cite the experience of Solzhenitsyn in the gulags or James

Jones and Norman Mailer, two veterans of the Pacific campaign in World War II. My own novels are usually set either in World War II or immediately afterwards, or in London or the Mediterranean where I spend much of my life.

But that is a long way from saying that a novel *must* be based on personal experience. Stephen Crane wrote one of the world's great war novels, *The Red Badge of Courage*, without ever leaving home. Owen Wister, a Philadelphia mandarin who studied music at the Conservatoire in Paris and visited Wyoming only for his health, wrote *The Virginian* in 1902, the book that created the image of cowboys and the Wild West that prevails to this day. Edgar Rice Burroughs wrote his endless Tarzan novels without originally knowing or subsequently learning anything about Africa. So from my point of view, the rule about writing from personal experience is a nonrule.

Here is a real rule: Never forget that your setting is just as important to the narrative as any of your characters. Without the *where*, your characters play out their parts in a vacuum. If you happen to live in New York, San Francisco, Los Angeles, Paris, Rome, Athens, Hong Kong, Alexandria, your *where* goes without saying and needs no explanation. Your background is ready-made. But only a minority of my readers will live in these places, and other locales must, as it were, work their passage. In *Humboldt's Gift* Saul Bellow had to spell out why part of his book was set in Chicago: Even a great city like Chicago has to have a *raison d'être*.

The setting has to be precise to a point where the reader could not conceive of the book's being set anywhere else. John Steinbeck's *Grapes of Wrath had* to be set in Oklahoma. The flight west from the land was the whole basis of the plot. Nelson Algren made Chicago fundamental to his themes, and Sinclair Lewis did the same for the Middle West. The novels of William Faulkner and Truman Capote and the plays of Tennessee Williams would make no sense if they were not set in the South.

I can give an even better example: A. J. Cronin's *The Stars Look Down* is a coal-mining novel set in the northeast of England, around Newcastle (which he calls Tynecastle). Richard

Llewellyn's *How Green Was My Valley* is a coal-mining novel set in the valleys of South Wales. The two settings are vital to the sense of the novels. If they were interchanged both books would lose all meaning.

If you do not live in one of the famous or glamorous places of the world, and I believe the overwhelming majority of you will be in that category, think very carefully about your setting. If you live in Des Moines or Carbondale, Illinois, or Munhall, Pennsylvania, or South Jordan, Utah, or a thousand other places and you are setting your novel there, that is OK. Providing, Des Moines, Carbondale, Munhall, South Jordan, and the rest are *vital to the narrative*. But if you are writing your characters and your story into those settings just because you happen to live there and know that Main Street and N.W. 36th Street connect at the Apollo movie theater, it isn't good enough. Your novel is doomed from the start because it lacks a base.

Those are strong words, but I have read too many manuscripts that have foundered on that issue alone. The setting *must* support plot and character and may even provide the theme. The success of *Peyton Place* resulted from the author's making her imaginary setting the worldwide symbol for smalltown decadence and amorality. The television series *Dallas* could have been set in Houston, I guess, but it was set in Dallas, and it has made Dallas a household word all over the television-watching world.

Are you afraid of trying to render settings to which you have never been exposed? You shouldn't give up on that account. Soak yourself in research, use your vacation time to travel—perhaps to a ski-resort, perhaps to the ocean, perhaps to some thermal spa. One of my students set her novel in a small town in Arkansas for no other reason than that was where she lived. The novel could have been transformed had she done nothing more than take off in her car and spend a few days at some spectacular mountain resort like Eureka Springs, Arkansas. Or if she had simply done some geographical homework.

If you have gone too far on your regional novel to turn back, I have a useful tip that I learned myself that can widen its appeal.

Make passing reference to the great world outside. If the novel is historical or semi-historical, set, say, in Texas in the first decade of this century, have some character wonder aloud, "What new shenanigan is that puppy in Washington, Teddy Roosevelt, getting up to now?" Or comment on the progress of the White Fleet. Or introduce in passing the assassination of President McKinley.

On a more up-to-date but specific time-setting, you can have a character switching off the television in disgust and wondering, "Are the Oakland A's going to win the World Series forever?" Or if the price of Scotch has gone up in his local liquor store, he may inquire sardonically, "I suppose we must have sold more grain to the goddamn Russians!"

Here is a rule about narrative prose that I discovered only after exposure to the lecture circuit: If it cannot be read aloud, it is probably no good. Gustave Flaubert wrote that if your prose does not follow the rhythms of the human lungs, it isn't worth a damn. That may be one of the reasons I am never sure I am flattered when people tell me I write the way I speak, even when they clearly intend it as a compliment—I don't like the sound of my own voice!

Charles Dickens, who was an actor *manqué* anyway, made a rewarding second career traveling through America and Britain reading from his own novels on the stage. Though none of us may ever be fortunate enough to be called upon to do that, we should nevertheless be well advised to try out our own narrative fiction aloud in front of the mirror. If you are pleased with the way your prose sounds, it is all the more likely your publisher will be pleased with what he reads.

One final rule: Don't be tyrannized by the idea that you have to begin at the beginning. When you sit down to write your book, write the first draft as you see it, without guidance from me or anyone else. Guidance and help come later.

Perhaps you will start at page 1 and continue through to the end before revising. Or perhaps not. When I begin a novel, there are some sequences that are absolutely clear in my mind, some are in shadows, and others will only emerge as the story progresses. Perhaps those clear sequences occur in the middle of the book, perhaps even at the end. If so, I write the last chapter first. Then I write the next most vivid sequence in my mind, and then the next. In the meantime my brain is stimulated by thoughts of how to fill the holes in between. Halfway through I make a stunning discovery: A sequence that I have conceived for the middle of the book will make a gripping beginning.

One of the advantages of this system is that it avoids what I call the "mountain-climbing" burden of fiction writing, or any other writing for that matter. Writing a book is like climbing a mountain. From the bottom the summit looks so far away, high in the clouds, perhaps invisible. The start is so slow, so little accomplished, so much to be done. The mountain-climber struggles to a ledge where he is briefly comfortable. He regards the sheer cliff above him, still to be climbed. How much nicer to rest, to unwrap the sandwich, and get out the thermos of coffee.

In writing, the equivalent lies in the comfort of revising, in perfecting what has already been written, rather than plunging once more into the unknown world of ideas and words.

My own system lightens the burden immensely. I am struggling up the sheer unexplored cliff-face of creative writing, and suddenly I am on a green plateau of a chapter or chapters I have already written, perhaps months earlier. Chapters, moreover, that gave me no trouble because they were so vivid in my mind when I wrote them. To be sure now, on revisiting, they may seem a little crude, unformed. But they are *there*. They don't have to be created, only revised.

But, as I said, either you see the task this way and decide it is a technique worth trying, or you don't. There may be better ways of climbing the mountain than your way, but if yours is the only way that you can see, stick with it. Of all the rules of writing fiction, the most ironclad of all is that no rule is absolutely ironclad.

3

THE ACT OF WRITING

I have just described a few of the basic rules and nonrules for writing fiction. A little later on I shall return to some of these rules and elaborate them into a constellation of suggested precepts and guidelines. For the moment, let's take a break and instead talk about that most mundane and vital of subjects, the actual process of writing.

Why so many textbooks on writing choose to ignore or gloss over this topic I cannot say. Perhaps it's too untheoretical to be attractive to the academic mind, too idiosyncratic, too resistant to being reduced to pat formulae. But I can assure you that very few topics are more interesting to professional writers, or more crucial to their performance.

The act of writing—as opposed to the craft of writing—is an odd mixture of continuous self-discipline and self-administered psychotherapy. Both activities are so necessary that, in the minds of some writers, they acquire almost mystical attributes. I know some novelists whose attitude toward their own work habits is nothing short of superstitious. Let one element in their daily routine go awry—a half hour's delay in getting started, a favorite working chair sent off to be reupholstered, the wrong kind of pencils in the pencil box—and they are virtually paralyzed as writers, unable to put two sentences together. I know one writer who has been so programmed over the years into writing in the morning that if he has an outside morning appointment, say, with his doctor, he has to have his wife escort him, otherwise he has vertigo and falls down on the sidewalk.

I suppose that firm discipline and incessant psychic self-help are really aspects of the same thing—strategies by which the writer copes with the worrisome mystery of his or her sources of inspiration. Writers don't really know *where* their ideas come from. They can't be sure when or how a needed idea will emerge, and, worse, they can't be absolutely sure that it ever will emerge. It's no wonder that writers sometimes give way to superstition, treating the processes of self-discipline and "psyching up" not merely as means of preparing the ground for the mysterious advent of an idea, but almost as acts of propitiation to unknown gods.

Whatever else they may be, discipline and psychic self-help are indispensable to the enterprise of imaginative writing. Writers meet these requirements in their own way. I can do no more than tell you some of the ways in which I meet them and hope that they may give you some insight into the *kind* of thing that may be required of you.

I get up about 6:00 or 6:15. I believe it was André Gide who declared that the greatest contribution made by the United States to civilized living was orange juice for breakfast. So I squeeze myself some orange juice, make some tea, listen to the news on the radio, and get to the typewriter. If I feel I am not fully awake or that my brain is rusty, I limber up with a few unnecessary letters to surprised friends.

With a faint background of classical music, I write without a break until 11:00 or 11:15. And that is my working day.

Toward the end of this working day I am on the alert for three warning signals to myself. Are my shoulder blades beginning to ache? That means it is time to stop. Am I beginning to make typing errors? I am usually a neat typer, so typing errors mean that my concentration is slipping. By now I am beginning to feel, physically, my brain emptying like an electric battery. Now my last preoccupation is whether I am coming to the end of a sequence, a point at which it would seem logical to end the day.

This I try as hard as I can to *avoid*. If I rise from my work with my day's train of thought completed, it means I have to start tomorrow with a new train of thought. And, come tomorrow morning, the train may not be in the station.

They say one should leave the dinner table still hungry. Similarly, I try to leave my typewriter wanting to write on. If I end my day's work in the middle of a theme, I can begin tomorrow where I left off today. By the time I come to the end of the theme, my brain will have become sufficiently alert so that I know exactly what to say next.

However, if I do find myself at a loss at the start of the day, I retype the last two pages that I typed the day before. I will invariably change and improve them and, in doing so, will have recovered the momentum to keep going.

I work 363 days a year (I take a day off at Christmas and, for some reason, Labor Day) and my average output is between 2,000 and 2,500 words a day. That sounds like a lot, but considering the revisions that lie ahead of me, perhaps three quarters of what I have written in my first draft will finish up in the wastepaper basket.

Before I start any page I put the date at the top right-hand corner. I do it in a kind of primitive code, so that my publisher won't see my tricks of the trade. If I write ten pages on February 8, the date will be on all ten pages as follows: ii/8.

In time my first draft is finished. I start on my second draft on May 12. I note that the page I am about to rewrite says ii/8. I write on my fresh virgin page, ii/8;v/12. I also check back on my calendar to see what I did on February 8, with whom I had lunch, what movie I saw in the afternoon, what letters I wrote. In other words, I try to recapture the mood, up or down, in which I wrote that page. After I retype the page I tear up and throw away the earlier draft.

I always make my second draft *two or three times as long as the first.* A first draft is nearly always the product of pell-mell enthusiasm. I hurried to get it all down and have skimped on just about everything—on atmosphere, characterization, plot, narrative, dialogue. I have described everything in one breath, as it were. But once I have the skeleton of the first draft, I now have the leisure to add the flesh, and after the flesh, the wardrobe.

Evelyn Waugh in his letters to fellow authors had a theme to which he referred time after time: *revision.* In 1951 he wrote to Nancy Mitford in Paris, "Revision is just as important as any other part of writing, and must be done *con amore*—with love. And as the English critic Reyner Heppenstall has said, "Waugh clearly never had anything to teach us except that a man may act like a fool and yet remain a master of English prose, perhaps the finest in this century."

By the end of the second draft I am cautiously optimistic about what I have achieved so far, but I realize that I still have a long way to go. I now get seriously to work, attacking the weakest links in the chain of events—those sequences that carry vestiges of first-draft crudeness. The months pass; Christmas comes and goes. The hieroglyphics at the top now seem to fill the whole page: ii/8;v/12;ix/24;xii/30.

I test myself with tricks. I take a page at random from the manuscript and rewrite it with one objective—make it a better page. It can be a sobering experience. What I thought, four months earlier, had been an excellent and praiseworthy page of prose proves to be full of flaws I missed before. But the good news is that as the work progresses, more and more of these pages pulled out at random seem to have hit just the mark I aimed at.

However, at some point you will find yourself going stale and, worse, running into a mental block, unable to go forward, backward, or sideways, only downward into mental potholes.

Staleness you must write yourself out of, no matter how uninspired or just plain lousy are the words you are putting on paper. Sooner or later you will struggle out of that Slough of Despond and later, reading back, you may discover that the words were not so lousy after all.

One way to combat staleness is to make sure that, linguistically speaking, you keep in shape. There are many ways a novelist's mind can train itself to be ready and agile for the novel-writing itself. I know novelists who limber up by typing off half a dozen letters to friends before settling down to serious business. (In 1981 Raymond Chandler's letters were posthumously collected and published. They amounted to a thick volume.) Others make notes to themselves.

Years ago, impressed by the brilliant way Vladimir Nabokov introduced poetry into *Lolita*, including some poetry in French, I sought to do the same thing myself. I am not a poet, but I am a pretty facile limericist and found that the discipline of verse invariably refreshed my brain for more serious work. The value in verse is that every word counts. Every beat to the bar has a word or syllable that slots into it. I tested myself by running my finger down the names of my students, picking the most complicated, and writing a limerick. One of these mythical students I shall call Joan Dengerbretson.

I wonder what Joan Dengerbretson
Would look like while wearing a Stetson?
Like a new Paul Revere?
Or perhaps Germaine Greer?
It's not a horse I would care to lay bets on.

Of a colleague I wrote:

Intellectually snobbish Miss Lawrence
Loves Bruckner, Brecht, Venice, and Florence.
As for sex I can't tell.
Perhaps with Lawrence Durell.
I know she holds me in abhorrence.

In a novel of mine as yet unfinished, my central character writes a limerick in French to the principal female character whose name is Kaari de Viese.

Etincellante Kaari de Viese,
Je trouve délicieuse et exquise.
Elle est intelligente,
Diligente, palpitante,
Et je n'oublirai jamais ses bises.

I have put verse to the test in several novels. The biggest challenge came in *Resort to War.* I had two teenage girls with a crush on each other corresponding from different private schools. Their letters took the form of Petrarchan sonnets. One problem was that, not being a poet, I shied away from comparison with sonnets like Keats' "On First Looking into Chapman's Homer," which read:

Oft have I travelled in the realms of gold
And many goodly states and kingdoms seen.
Round many western islands have I been
Which bards in fealty to Apollo hold.
Oft of one wide expanse have I been told
That deep-browed Homer ruled as his demesne
Yet never did I breathe its pure serene
'Till I heard Chapman speak out loud and bold.
Then felt I like some watcher of the skies
When a new planet swims into his ken;
Or like stout Cortez when with eagle eyes
He star'd at the Pacific—and all his men
Look'd at each other with a wild surmise,
Silent, upon a peak in Darien.

That, of course, was far too hard an act to follow. The meter and verse of the Petrarchan sonnet is precise. The rhyme proceeds, *a, b, b, a, a, c, c, a, d, e, d, e, d, e* over the course of fourteen lines. But I had a way out to cushion and even justify my inferiority as a classical poet. I was dealing with two impressionable young girls whose deficiencies could be excused. Here was one written by Paula to Mireille.

Flaccid in the sun, the sky without Mireille
But I remain mysteriously serene.
On Vassar's lawns she lies with me unseen
Not there but here our Vallée des Merveilles.
Ni crépuscule ni l'aube n'attend notre douce réveille.
We tread our path where no one else has been.
There is a world of in-between
Where only loving girls can stay.
And bountifully love full well.
Barefoot and warm where fountains play,
And all the rest can go to hell.

The point is not in the quality or lack of quality of the sonnet, but the exercise that proved so stimulating to the formation of the narrative and to the momentum of the author. You can't really go stale if you are genuinely interested in the problems you set for yourself.

A mental block is harder. One of my techniques is to go around the obstacle altogether and move to some other sequence in the book that is clearer in my mind. Later I will come back to the obstacle. By then I often find that the problem has solved itself.

Another way around the mental block is to change the scene altogether, perhaps to a new scene you will have to invent. Let us suppose Jim is about to give himself up to the police after murdering his girl friend. You have no idea how to resolve the scene in the police station. Don't. Flash back to the first time Jim met his girl friend. Or switch to a cocktail bar where a couple of Jim's friends are getting drunk on dry martinis. Switch to Jim's daughter graduating from high school. While you are pussyfooting with these peripheral scenes, the problem of the police station scene is gradually clarifying in your head.

Yet another way of breaking the block is to pick up and reread your favorite authors. After all, these were the authors who inspired you to write in the first place. Somewhere in their narrative you will find a key, perhaps a sequence, perhaps a mere sentence that will make you exclaim, "Of course!" and you rush back to the manuscript. I am not talking in any way of plagiarism. You simply will have noticed that the author has faced a situation parallel to your own and how he has gotten out of it. He has shown the signpost for which you have been searching.

One thing you do *not* do; if you are stale or going through a block, you don't say, "OK, I will take the day off, fix the storm windows, go to a movie, put the whole damn book out of my mind and return fresh to the typewriter tomorrow." You will go back to the typewriter the following day, but you won't be fresh. The block will not have gone away. It will be denser. Before it only needed application. Today it will need blasting. Furthermore, it will encourage a second day off. And a third. And the ultimate result will be that you no longer have the impetus to write the book at all.

One of the wisest men I ever met in the literary business was the agent Max Wilkinson, one-time story editor to Sam Goldwyn and now living in semiretirement. He had delivered a book of mine to the publisher and everyone was happy. My bank account looked good, my brain was empty. I said, "Max, I'm tired. I am going to take six weeks off and go on a cruise. I won't even take my typewriter. I shall read books, catch marlin, and get myself a noble suntan."

Wilkinson chewed on his spectacles and said, "Hmmmm. Sounds like a pretty good idea. You've got a problem, however. By the time you get back you will have forgotten how to write at all. It will take you another six weeks to get back into the rhythm. Can you afford it?"

He was right of course and, swearing, I found myself back at the typewriter next morning. Which, of course, was just what he intended.

In other words, practice is as important to a writer as it is to any other gifted person. John McEnroe seems to be playing tournament tennis every day. Why should he need to practice?

But he still practices every morning. The same applies to a concert pianist, a ballet dancer, an opera singer. I find that even two days away from the typewriter makes my mental joints creak. I have driven across America and Europe, but I always made sure to keep a journal every day.

4

PLOT: THE BASIS OF THE NOVEL

There is only one plot to any and every novel—good or bad, serious or funny. The plot is the struggle of your central character against the apparently ineluctable approach of disaster. Consider your central character, determine the form of the disaster, and you have the basis of your novel.

That is about as large a statement as you will find in these pages, so I won't apologize if I go on to contradict myself several times. Plots are frequently the most unwelcome part of the novelist's task. You may love forming characters. You relish putting good dialogue on to paper. You enjoy the flow of your narrative. But plot. . .?

When I wrote *Bikini Beach* for Mc-Graw Hill, my editor there was the late John Starr. I walked into his office one day and found him raging: "Plots! Plots! Plots! Why do novelists hate plots so much? I don't mind a novel that doesn't have much of a plot. I don't mind novels with no plot at all. But here I am with a manuscript from Ernie Gann that has an excellent plot, and he is running away from it."

Max Wilkinson once said to me, "Plots are really only devices for making readers want to know what's going to happen next. Let's suppose that you create three young women: one

American, one English, one French. Set them on the Riviera. Follow their intertwining fortunes over the course of a year against the background of the Mediterranean—the beaches, the casinos, the hill villages, the beautiful people, the gigolos. Make one girl's experience a happy one, another tragic, and perhaps have the third one drown or commit suicide. Technically speaking, is this a novel with a plot? Does it really matter, so long as it keeps the reader turning the pages?"

As a result of this good advice, I sat down and wrote *Giselle*, which was published by Putnam in the United States, McGibbon Hart-Davies in England, and translated into several languages. Was it a plotted novel? Yes and no. It wasn't plotless, but it certainly wasn't dominated by a single central plot.

So, the novel writer is faced with two interchangeable alternatives: either to write a centrally plotted novel or to write what I will call a sequential novel, in which event follows event in a looser, sometimes contrapuntal way. Scott Fitzgerald wrote both. I would call *Tender Is the Night* a sequential novel, and *The Great Gatsby*, a novel that is plotted precisely from the first word to the last.

Most of my plots simply have evolved. Rarely have they struck like a flash of lightning, and even more rarely did they result from elaborate preplanning. And yet I am by no means sure that my rather relaxed approach to plotting has been the best one. In fact, it was not until my last novel that I really discovered (and that by accident) how interesting it could be to construct a story with a central plot carefully worked out in advance.

I had never written an outline for a novel before for the very good reason that publishers don't like them, read them with reluctance, and say, "I'd like to read the book when it's finished." A nonfiction book can be sold on an outline or even an idea, but the publisher of fiction can have only a partial idea of merit of a novel until he reads it all. However, a suggestion, which I offer with caution, is to write yourself an outline first.

Knowing I would have to set my new novel aside while

writing this book, I set it down in outline form *for myself alone*. It began as a twenty-page outline, then became thirty pages, then forty pages, and then ninety. But the curious thing was this: As it progressed it became less and less of a sequential novel and more and more of a plotted novel. The restricted form of the outline, the elimination of the atmosphere, dialogue, characterization that are essential to a novel, enabled me to see it as a skeleton, to see the end at the same time as I saw the beginning.

And from this I suddenly realized something about centrally plotted novels that I had never fully understood before. Namely, that from the writer's point of view, the plot frequently begins backward, in the last chapter, and proceeds to the beginning. The death of Gatsby and Daisy's rationalizations at the end proceed to the huge house party this mysterious man gives in the opening chapter.

The ending of Frederic Forsyth's *Day of the Jackal*, one of the most brilliant I have ever read, is thrilling and surprising when you read it. Yet when you stop to think about it, it was also inevitable. De Gaulle, we know, wasn't murdered; the assassination attempt had to be foiled. The only real question was *how*. And it was to answer that one question that Forsyth wrote the whole rest of the book. Though we do not quite realize it while we are reading *Day of the Jackal*, we are being propelled in a straight line toward that final, climactic scene.

The very idea of plot implies a climax, and in centrally plotted novels, the major climax almost always coincides with the end of the book. In such novels the climax should begin quietly in the first paragraph and grow and grow until the blockbuster at the end.

All this seems so obvious, yet writers—even some of the greatest—are constantly giving way to the temptation to go on writing after the major climax has been reached. Shakespeare goofed in *Romeo and Juliet*. The climax is the double duel between Tybalt and Mercutio and then Tybalt and Romeo. I myself think the rest of the play is anticlimactic. And I couldn't be all that wrong because the same applies to *West Side Story*, which is based on *Romeo and Juliet*. The climax is the knife fight, after the which the story simply tails away.

The climax of Tolstoy's *War and Peace* is the Battle of Borodino. The climax of *Gone With the Wind* is the burning of Atlanta. The climax of *Treasure Island* is the battle for the stockade. All three novels flag afterward through the sheer weariness of both author and reader.

I can't suggest what Shakespeare, Tolstoy, or Margaret Mitchell might have done to correct this. I made the same mistake in *Giselle*. I described a Monaco Grand Prix in the minutest detail over the course of three chapters, moving from the racing cars to the fears of the drivers' girl friends to some human drama, a little comedy, a bit of sex, and back to the cars, until the hero crashes and is burned to death. That ends Part I of my novel. The second half is a bore. What annoys me in retrospect is that the error was avoidable. By juggling the sequences I could have made the race the climax to the end of the book. And my publisher should have spotted it as quickly as I should have done. The blame rested with both of us.

Ah, well. There is no such thing as a perfect novelist. Or, thank heaven, an all-knowing publisher.

Not all climaxes are final climaxes and, for that matter, not all novels are centrally plotted. Insofar as centrally plotted novels are concerned, the story line progresses like the jagged line graph doctors use to chart a rising fever. Each peak on the graph represents a kind of climax in its own right, a moment of particular excitement or emotional intensity in the story. As a general rule (though there can be many variations), the peaks get higher as the story unfolds, the highest peak always representing the final climax.

But this isn't necessarily true of sequential novels. A picaresque novel such as James Clavell's *Shogun* or Henry Fielding's *Tom Jones* may consist of a succession of climaxes all of more or less the same intensity. There is no special building toward a final burst of fireworks, only a highly diverting journey toward some sort of resolution of the main characters' basic problems. In such novels, most of the fun lies, as they say in the airline ads, "in getting there."

If your novel contains more than one plot—either parallel major plots or a major plot interwoven with subplots—choreographing its structure can become much more difficult. But the results may be worth the extra effort. It can be boring for the reader—and for the writer too—to be constantly obliged to gnaw on the protagonists' central problem. Sometimes it's a relief to be able to get away and worry about someone else's problems for a change.

A plot may serve to indicate some ultimate destination toward which the story is leading, as in a problem to be overcome or a mystery to be solved, and thereby whet the reader's appetite to find out how we are going to get to that destination. Or it may merely serve as a vehicle for setting up a series of incidents so interesting in themselves that the reader won't much care where he is being led. It really doesn't matter, *so long as the reader keeps turning those pages*.

I suppose I could go on and on about the art of plotting. Certainly it seems to be a matter that fascinates the authors of textbooks on creative writing, and you even can find books that purport to give you the 20 (or 50 or 100, depending on the author's analysis) "basic plots" from which all other plots are supposed to be derived. But in the end, I think Max Wilkinson was right: Plot is merely one of the devices writers use—among many others—to make readers want to go on reading.

What's really at issue is how well you can tell a story. Plot may be a useful, even necessary, element in making you an interesting literary storyteller, but plot is a long way from being the only, or even the most important, element. Put it this way: Well-plotted novels can easily fail; well-written novels almost never fail.

Plot aside, what constitutes good novel writing? Well, for one thing, your ability to recreate the physical world in words.

As we shall see.

5

DESCRIPTION: DETAILS AND FEELINGS

Writers describe the world as they see it. Most of us are prisoners of our own personal experiences. Our points of view mold our novels, and if we succeed, we widen the reader's experience of life. Novelists have frequently portrayed the ages in which they lived more vividly than historians. Karl Marx wrote that "Dickens and Thackeray have issued to the world more political and social truths than have been uttered by all the professional politicians, publicists, and moralists put together." His sidekick Engels said he learned more from Honoré Balzac about post-revolutional France "than from all the professed historians, economists, and statisticians of the period together."

Let us study one subject as seen through the eyes of two of the world's great writers. The subject is the River Thames, the writers: Charles Dickens and Joseph Conrad. Dickens is a landlubber and a child of the winding, narrow, dirty streets of London. To him water is an enemy, sucking him down, concealing the evidence, making him seasick. Joseph Conrad is a sailor who has grown up with the blue horizon as the limit of his vision. Here is the River Thames of Charles Dickens in *Our Mutual Friend:*

"Hallo! Steady!" cried Eugene (he had recovered immediately on embarking), as they bumped heavily against a pile; and then in a lower voice reversed his late apostrophe by remarking ("I wish the boat of my honourable and gallant friend may be endowed with philanthropy enough *not* to turn bottom-upward and extinguish us!) Steady, steady! Sit close, Mortimer. Here's the hail again. See how it flies, like a troop of wild cats, at Mr. Riderhood's eyes!"

Indeed he had the full benefit of it, and it so mauled him, though he bent his lead low and tried to present nothing but the mangy cap to it, that he dropped under the lee of a tier of shipping, and they lay there until it was over. The squall had come up, like a spiteful messenger before the morning; there followed in its wake a ragged tier of light which ripped the dark clouds until they showed a great grey hole of day.

They were all shivering, and everything about them seemed to be shivering; the river itself, craft, rigging, sails, such early smoke as there yet was on the shore. Black with wet, and altered to the eye by white patches of hail and sleet, the huddled buildings looked lower than usual, as if they were cowering, and had shrunk with the cold. Very little life was to be seen on either bank, windows and doors were shut, and the staring black and white letters upon wharves and warehouses "looked," said Eugene to Mortimer, "like inscriptions over the graves of dead businesses."

As they glided slowly on, keeping under the shore, and sneaking in and out among the shipping, by back-alleys of water, in a pilfering way that seemed to be their boatman's normal manner of progression, all the objects among which they crept were so huge in contrast with their wretched boat as to threaten to crush it. Not a ship's hull, with its rusty iron links of cable run out of hawse-holes long discoloured with the iron's rusty tears, but seemed to be there with a fell intention. Not a figure-head but had the menacing look of bursting forward to run them down. Not a sluice gate, or a painted scale upon a post or wall, showing the depth of water, but seemed to hint, like the dreadfully facetious Wolf in bed in Grandmamma's cottage, "That's to drown *you* in, my dears!" Not a lumbering black barge, with its cracked and blistered side impending over them, but seemed to suck at the river with a thirst for sucking them under. And everything so

> vaunted the spoiling influences of water—discoloured copper, rotten wood, honey-combed stone, green dank deposit—that the after-consequences of being crushed, sucked under, and drawn down, looked as ugly to the imagination as the main event.

What superb writing! "Inscriptions over the graves of dead businesses" . . . "back-alleys of water." This is the River Thames of fear. Now listen to Joseph Conrad's river:

> The old river in its broad-reach rested unruffled at the decline of the day, after ages of good service done to the race that peopled its banks, spread out in the tranquil dignity of a waterway leading to the uttermost ends of the earth. We looked at the venerable stream not in the vivid flush of a short day that comes and departs for ever, but in the august light of abiding memories. And indeed nothing is easier for a man who has, as the phrase goes, "followed the sea" with reverence and affection, than to evoke the great spirit of the past upon the lower reaches of the Thames. The tidal current runs to and fro in its unceasing service, crowded with memories of men and ships it has borne to the rest of home or to the battles of the sea. It had known and served all the men of whom the nation is proud, from Sir Francis Drake to Sir John Franklin, knights all, titled and untitled—the great knights-errant of the sea. It had borne all the ships whose names are like jewels flashing in the night of time, from the *Golden Hind* returning with her round flanks full of treasure, to be visited by the Queen's Highness and thus pass out of the gigantic tale, to the *Erebus* and *Terror*, bound on other conquests—and that never returned. It had known the ships and the men. They had sailed from Deptford, from Greenwich, from Erith—the adventurers and the settlers; kings' ships and the ships of men on 'Change; captains, admirals, the dark "interlopers" of the Eastern trade, and the commissioned "generals" of East India fleets. Hunters for gold or pursuers of fame, they all had gone out on that stream, bearing the sword, and often the torch, messengers of the might within the land, bearers of a spark from the sacred fire. What greatness had not floated on the ebb of that river into the mystery of an unknown

> earth! . . . The dreams of men, the seed of commonwealths, the germs of empires.
>
> The sun set; the dusk fell on the stream, and lights began to appear along the shore. The Chapman lighthouse, a three-legged thing erect on a mud-flat, shone strongly. Lights of ships moved in the fairway—a great stir of lights going up and going down. And farther west on the upper reaches the place of monstrous town was still marked ominously in the sky, a brooding gloom in sunshine, a lurid glare under the stars.

Curious that Conrad should have given us that joyous picture of the Thames in, of all novels, *The Heart of Darkness*.

These passages illustrate two important points about good literary description: it is constructed not out of voluminous summaries, but out of small, significant details; and it conveys not merely the physical scene, but the author's feelings about it.

If an artist were to have tried to paint a riverscape based on Dickens' description, he might well have come up with something that caught Dickens' mood perfectly and yet be nothing like the image Dickens had in mind when he wrote the passage. "Fair enough!" Dickens would probably have said, "That's all I wanted." For Dickens knew that you can almost never imaginatively recreate the essence of anything by cataloguing all its component parts. Even the human memory itself doesn't work that way. Try, for example, to remember (or better yet, make a sketch of) the complete contents of a room in the house or apartment of one of your friends. You'll be lucky if you can inventory a hundredth of the things in that room, and luckier still if you can describe their precise shapes, colors, and positions with respect to one another. Yet you nevertheless have a vivid impression of that room—an impression made up not of exhaustive memories, but of a few sharply remembered details that for you characterize the place.

Literary description operates on almost the same principle as memory. A handful of details—parts that stand for the whole—are everything. Go beyond that handful and you accomplish nothing. In fact, you will quickly begin to bore both your reader and yourself and finish by actually weakening the power of your description.

And how can you be sure that you've hit on just the details that will be significant to the reader, that will so trigger his imagination that he can supply all the other things you've left unsaid? I don't know of any good way to answer that. All I can say is that somehow it just comes to you and it isn't as hard as it sounds. Perhaps one reason why is that what is significant to you is likely to seem significant to the reader as well. Don't ask me why; I suppose it's just that we're all more similar than we like to think.

In order for *you* to find a detail significant, you must have some feeling about it, some personal response to it. It would be too much to ask that you fully understand its *meaning*. What specific meaning did Dickens see in that "lumbering black barge with its cracked and blistered sides"? What specific meaning did Conrad see in the fact that "the Chapman lighthouse, a three-legged thing erect on a mud flat, shone strongly"? All we can say for sure is that these details were not only genuine parts of the physical scenes being described but were closely associated with attitudes of the authors—in Dickens' case, an attitude of fear and dislike; in Conrad's, of exultant nostalgia. And because they seemed significant to the authors, they seem significant to us.

I don't mean to minimize the difficulty. It's obviously one thing to *extract* just the right details from a scene you've actually witnessed and about which you feel strongly; it's quite another thing to *implant* significant details into a scene you've just made up in your head.

At first glance, it might seem that whereas the first is mainly a matter of selection, the second is an act of creative imagination. That's not quite the way it works in practice. Novelists are forever on the lookout for just those vivid little details that they can lift out of their real-life contexts, store away in memory or (better) a notebook, and later get into their novels. Novelists and magpies have a lot in common.

Show me a man or woman walking along the street wearing earphones and I will show you a person who can never be a novelist. He and she are wiping out the world around them, the same world that is the food and drink of the novelist. Everything fascinates the novelist, including the person along the street with earphones, because that person is so alien. The person will surely appear somewhere in the author's next novel.

The man who admires a pretty girl in the street—after the admiration of face or form, what does he look for? The presence or absence of a wedding ring. On that depends the degree of hope that springs eternal.

In Kansas City Airport among a milling crowd waiting for missed connections, I saw a man I knew to be an Englishman. How did I know? By the sleeves of his jacket. American tailors simply sew buttons to the sleeve. British tailors make buttonholes for the buttons.

What do we remember about Alexander the Great? Just a sigh. Because he had no more worlds to conquer. What symbolizes the spirit of England at the Battle of Trafalgar? Not Nelson's signal expecting all Englishmen this day to do their duty, but the response of one Jack Tar reading the message: "What the bloody hell does he expect us to do!"

Alexander Solzhenitsyn is only one example of a master of detail, but he may arguably be supreme. Among the many aspects of his genius is that he is a brilliant journalist. He observes everything. He can write a thousand-page novel, a monumental history, and a 500-word short story with equal facility. One of his short novellas called *For the Good of the Party,* is about how a group of university students decide to build a theater for themselves with their bare hands. The commissars wait until they have completed it and then take it over "for the good of the party." At one point Solzhenitsyn writes of how the KGB men arrive in town by train. Everyone knew that they were KGB men because they all wore green fedoras: There must have been a consignment that had just arrived in Moscow because the KGB always got the first pick of everything. What to many would be a detail beneath notice was to Solzhenitsyn the key to the whole inhuman regimentation of Soviet society, a green fedora.

I suggest that anyone writing a novel should turn to Solzhenitsyn for ideas, tricks, and literary surprises because his writing is full of all those things. If you have not already done so, *Lenin in Zurich* (New York: Farrar, Straus & Giroux, 1976, tr. H.T. Willetts), a short biographical novel, may be the ideal one to consult first. It begins with Lenin on a train with his comrades traveling to western Europe from Siberia. Lenin,

> ... carrying a basket of subversive literature and a letter with a plan for *Iskra** in invisible ink, chose that, of all times to be too clever, too conspiratorial. The rule is to change trains en route, but they had forgotten that the other train would pass through Tserskoye Selo, and were detained by the gendarmes as suspicious persons. Luckily the police with their salutary Russian sluggishness gave them time to get rid of the basket, and took the letter at its face value because they could not be bothered to hold it over a flame....

Consider the image of a "basket" of subversive literature, the "salutary sluggishness" of the gendarmes. My professional curiosity popped up here. *Gendarmes?* I checked my Russian-English dictionary that I find to be a useful part of my reference library. "Police" in Russian is *Polizier,* and I saw no word for *gendarme* either in the English-Russian or Russian-English sections. Solzhenitsyn was jocularly using Tsarist affectation.

That is the beginning of *Lenin in Zurich.* Here is how the book ends, with Lenin and his cohorts on the way back to join the Russian Revolution:

> Lenin put on his iron-heavy quilted greatcoat, and Radek the thin summer coat in which he ran around all through the winter, his pockets crammed with books.... He filled his pipe, and had his

*Iskra is the Russian word for "Spark," the title Lenin selected for his new magazine.

> matches ready.... Radek, light-footed and pleased with himself danced about like an adolescent....

Consider the detail in every word—the "iron-heavy quilted greatcoat." The blinding vividness of Radek in a thin summer coat in winter, "his pockets crammed" with books, pleased with himself, dancing about like an adolescent. Radek again:

> "My hands itch, my tongue itches! I can't wait for the wide-open spaces of Russia, can't wait to go agitating!"
>
> And, letting Lenin go first, holding a match ready to strike in the corridor, he said, "It comes to this, Vladimir Ilyitch; six months from now we will either be ministers or we will be hanged."

This is sheer theater. Radek letting the master precede him. Even the act of holding the match ready and letting Lenin pass before lighting his pipe in the corridor, gives us in half a sentence a glowing image of obsequiousness and of *movement* in the word "corridor." Anyone in a corridor is in transit elsewhere.

Even now, Solzhenitsyn is not finished with us. He carries us to the very last words. We have the advantage of hindsight. Radek has no such advantage. See how limited is his vision. He sees them as mere "ministers." The mere mortal does not yet conceive that the man in the iron-heavy quilted greatcoat striding ahead of him is the man who would change the twentieth century. Perhaps his lack of foresight is just as well—Solzhenitsyn was thinking of this too, as he wrote, for Stalin clapped Radek in jail during the purges of the 1930s.

So far we have been dwelling on the importance of significant details. But what about insignificant details? Should they all be banished from our narrative prose? The answer is yes, most of them should be banished, *but not all of them*.

Think about it for a moment. Imagine that I am sitting at the bar of a saloon in Flemington, New Jersey, writing notes. Overhead, shiny new electric fans are clicking. They are just about the only new things in the place. The barstools are frayed. If the boss doesn't get some fresh linoleum tiles to replace those that have disappeared, some drunken customer is going to trip and sue him. Someone has put a quarter into the jukebox, which has burst into sound with country music: "*Oh, I never wenta bed with an ugly woman, but I sho' woke up with a few. . . .*" A large round plate with an illustration of the American flag and the dates 1776–1976 stands, crooked, behind the bottles. The person who used the ashtray before I arrived wore pale pink lipstick. A woman sitting near me, drinking a beer with a rye chaser, has a tattoo on her left shoulder. Outside a convoy of cars rushes by, klaxons blaring, and trailing white wedding streamers. . . .

What does all this add up to? Nothing really. Air. But air is what every novel needs. A five-hundred-word newspaper report must make every word tell. A five-thousand word magazine article requires the regular pause for air with an anecdote. Written as tightly as a newspaper story, it would choke the reader. A 65,000-word novel needs air in the same proportion.

There were perhaps a dozen people in that saloon, and no two would see it in the same way. In fact they probably didn't see it at all. But I saw it for the air it gave me between sequences in some future novel I may or may not write.

Every facet and thought in the novel must deepen and clarify the background. One of the manuscripts I read involved a railroad line running through the neighborhood, and a train. One of the most beautiful, melancholy, and, alas, dying sounds in the world is the hoot of a train. I penciled in the margin a note to the student: "Why isn't the train whistling?"

You are not merely describing background, you are describing your protagonist's perception of the background. The same setting might convey two entirely different moods to two different characters. The hospital, the wards, the waiting rooms can be restful to one character and claustrophobic to another. It might be a place of efficient precision, of mausoleumlike coolness, of computerized inhumanity.

In your hospital one character stands in the waiting room, unconsciously hearing the ticking of the wall clock. To him the clock is ticking lazily and out of rhythm. The doctor and the nurse don't hear the clock at all. Why bring this up? Because it sets a mood of uncertainty, insecurity, imbalance. If the doctor and the nurse don't notice the ticking, will they notice anything? Or are they robots? Human computers? And if they are, what care will the person in the hospital receive? A character notices that the doctor is young and wearing open-toed sandals. What kind of doctor is this, for heaven's sake? Can one trust such a person? Another character is going mad for lack of reading. Someone had left behind the local newspaper and the character has read it from cover to cover, comics to crossword, but the waiting is still not over, the waiting is still not over, the waiting. . . . Nothing to read. . . .

Many of you will be nondrinkers and nonsmokers. Bully for you! But this is also likely to mean you never think about drinking or smoking and in consequence might eliminate the weed and the grape from your consciousness while you are writing your novel. This could be a mistake, giving you that much less air for your narrative.

In the theater the process is called "business." A cigarette can be stubbed out in anger. An empty pack can be crushed in the hand and thrown away in frustration. At the end of a cocktail party, ashtrays can be upended into a wastepaper basket with a pleasing swishing sound. (Noel Coward uses this trick amusingly in his play *Present Laughter.*) A pipe can be tapped and knocked and returned to a rack with a dozen other pipes. A cigar can be meticulously lit with a wooden match. All such pauses in the narrative give the reader a breather, a chance to catch up.

Take a girl.

There has to be more to her than "a girl."

A red-headed girl. Better. And. . . ?

A red-headed girl smoking a small black cheroot.

All at once, we see the girl. Further description may even, given the context, be unnecessary.

Similarly with drink. In *The Thin Man*, one knows vividly what Nick Charles is like by the number of dry martinis he drinks. More "business": A professional Army officer, overwhelmed by humiliation for some defeat, hurls his glass of bourbon at the portrait on the wall of the president of the United States.

Gavin Lyall, perhaps my favorite English suspense writer, begins a novel something like this: "My Cessna 99 spiraled down toward the bleak face of the Himalaya. With my right hand, I desperately tried to bring the aircraft back under control, while my left tried to keep my dry martini from spilling. . . ."

And as for the opportunities offered by the hangover! Even eliminating *The Lost Weekend* and *Hangover Square*, one could still complete a fat anthology on the hangover in literature.

I was sitting on the floor recently, cleaning my shoes. It occurred to me that shoe cleaning is one of the most macho of all acts. Men who have known military service tend to have a fetish about beautifully shined shoes. They spit into the shoe polish to make the right moist mix. They select the cleaning rags with care. They tend to whistle while they polish. They hold the shoe at arm's length to appreciate the gleam. As a gesture they will also polish women's shoes, which is not easy because women's shoes come in all sorts of colors and there is often less leather than there is air. Women tend not to be able to shine shoes, so they reciprocate by sewing the missing buttons onto men's shirts.

And rain. What mileage can be derived from a downpour—the business with umbrellas, galoshes, wet hair, soaking clothes. I noticed in one of my fiction classes that in all the manuscripts I read, not a single raindrop fell. The students had not thought of rain. Or sunshine.

I am not being funny when I add that literary air also means temperature. The reader must know at all times what the weather is like—whether the protagonists are hot or cold, sweating or shivering. The sky, the sun, the moon, the rain, the slush are all essential to a reader's understanding of the novel.

A special category of "air" is gratuitous expert information, the kind of useless nuggets of hard fact that, for some reason, we novel readers adore. Take the following exceedingly boring paragraph from a book on photomechanics that I pulled down from a shelf and opened at random:

> If we ascribe lenslike properties to the apertures of halftone screens, we must also ascribe to them a property possessed by every lens—a definite focal length. This is the so-called screen distance which must prevail between the cover-glass of the screen and the photographic surface during halftone exposures with glass crossline screens.

Huh? But suppose those words are being uttered by Helga Birkenmeier, photomechanical expert in the West German National Security Bureau, and what she is telling Bill Barkle of the CIA is that the West Germans have invented a process by which Soviet nuclear submarines can be photographed on the Atlantic seabed with an instrument no bigger than a cigarette. In this context, the words carry meaning even if one cannot understand them. Like the recitative in opera that isn't music, like an abstract painting one cannot understand, or incomprehensible poetry, they have a queer sort of life of their own. They are *tactile* words that can almost be rubbed between finger and thumb.

Harold Robbins applies this tactility to the subject of money in *The Carpetbaggers*, Judith Krantz to high fashion in *Scruples*, Barbara Taylor Bradford to department stores in *A Woman of Substance*, Dick Francis to horse-racing in all his books. A reader vicariously enjoys being let in by the stage door to subjects he knows nothing about, into the technicalities, the jargon, the minutiae.

It needs a certain amount of homework but it is rarely difficult. If you want to describe, say, a hysterectomy, or a cholostomy, ask your doctor for a technical description. He will be pleased to show off his knowledge and won't charge you. If your story deals with corporation law, ask your lawyer. If you are writing about the used-car business ask your used-car dealer.

This kind of technical juggling need not be confined to paragraph-length descriptions; often it can be used to great effect in a very few words. It appears that Abraham Lincoln did *not*, after hearing complaints of General Grant's drinking, say, "Send him a case of the same brand," but it remains one of my favorite historical antecdotes. In fiction the reader can get a clearer idea of a character by knowing that character's tastes and preferences.

A rich college girl may be described simply as "a rich college girl." But a college girl wearing a Lacoste shirt, Gloria Vanderbilt jeans, and Gucci loafers presents a much clearer picture. She *has* to be rich. And the precision of the description prompts us to supply other imaginary details. She is probably spoiled, suffers from post-puberty acne, and is waiting for one of her family trusts to be freed. We can almost see her sorority ring and the ivy on the college walls.

Compare the following two interpretations of the same scene:

> Hank was a prudent man. He checked that his car doors were locked, left the parking lot, and entered the terminal. At the insurance counter he lit a cigarette, bought a flight insurance policy, and took his place in line at the ticket counter.
>
> Hank was a prudent man. He checked that the doors of his Chevrolet Impala were locked before he entered Newark International Air Terminal. At the insurance counter, he lit a Marlboro with a book match, bought a $1.25 flight insurance policy, and then took his place at the Lufthansa ticket counter.

Of course, this is a practice that can be overdone: James Bond with his Mark Cross luggage and other accessories, overdoes it flagrantly. Overdone, the narrative can read like an advertising brochure. But well done, it can be used as an excellent shortcut to a reader's understanding of the character. A Jack Daniels man *is* different from a Glen Livet man.

Just as in writing about sex and using four-letter words, it is up to the author to make sure that the use of brand names is not overdone. Once the right balance is struck it can clarify the reader's mind in a flash, an *Augenblick*. The aim is to cut time and explanation to a minimum.

The reference to sex and four-letter words brings me to the second great branch of narrative prose. Up to this point we have been concerned almost solely with the kind of prose that describes things, people, and their attributes more or less at rest. But what about that other kind of prose that describes people and things in *action?* Although it may be a mistake to assume that action prose is necessarily the most important kind of prose that a novelist must master, it is usually true that no novel can do without it.

6

ACTION AND DIALOGUE

There are two sorts of action passages in fiction: those that describe action that occurs at the time the central narrative is supposed to be taking place—the narrative "now"—and those that describe action that occurred at some previous time. In terms of dramatic impact, they are as different as chalk and cheese. Description of past action is mere history, a summation of bygone events that may qualify as information crucial to our understanding of the present situation, but that has only marginal dramatic value in itself. Ninety-nine percent of the drama in fiction results from action that occurs in the narrative "now." (Please note, by the way, that this concept of "now" may be a bit flexible. For as long as it lasts, a flashback can be considered almost as much "now" as is the time frame that encloses the central narrative.)

It's hard to avoid presenting *any* summaries of past action in novel writing, but you must be aware that these summaries will be essentially flat passages. Thus, in general, it's a good idea to keep them as short as possible and to try to position them as artfully as you can. For example, a summary of certain past events sandwiched between two high-tension "now" action scenes might just provide the kind of breather that could show off the two "now" scenes to best advantage.

"Now" action comes in two basic forms: physical action and dialogue. And of these, dialogue is certainly the more difficult to master and may be the more important. I say this because scenes of physical action—provided they are well thought out in advance and are written briskly, with strong verbs and a minimum of adjectives and adverbs—are fairly easy to carry off. Certainly they are important, for they can provide your story with many, if not most, of its exciting climaxes. Yet they cannot by themselves sustain the story itself. A story that consisted of nothing but descriptions of physical action would be both thin and boring. The kind of action that gives a novel most of its meaning and emotional texture—the solid cake for which scenes of physical action may be merely the frosting—is the interpersonal give and take that is best expressed in dialogue.

So most of this chapter is going to be about dialogue rather than about the altogether simpler subject of physical action, but before I turn to the subject of dialogue proper, I'd like to say something about a couple of difficult matters that encompass both physical action and fictional conversation.

Two of the toughest problems in fiction writing are how to write explicit sex and how to handle four-letter words. Both are not only commonplace in fiction, but are almost demanded by the reader. One of my novels was edited by a senior editor for a distinguished New York publishing house, and this gentleman insisted, against my own judgment, on my putting in more sex and more sex and more sex. I don't know who was right. The book did well and was translated into several languages, but many critics were offended by the excessive use of explicit sex, and you can judge my personal opinion by the fact that I am not naming the book, the editor, or the publishing house.

The lesson I learned, however, benefited me in subsequent books. The lesson is this, look upon both sex and obscenities as literary capital, to be spent with the greatest care. Once the agreed capital has been spent, use no more. If you simply lard sex and cuss-words into the text without specific reason, you will soon offend the reader. I myself was thoroughly offended by the ear-splitting four-letter words which seemed to constitute the only dialogue of the movie *Saturday Night Fever.* Its defenders say, "But that is how people talk." That is no defense. *On the Waterfront*, written by Budd Schulberg, was as tough a novel as has been written in modern times, but it contained no four-letter words. That the censorship of the time might have banned them is beside the point. The language was implied, and the book lost nothing. Various censorships did not diminish the sexual passions of *The Brothers Karamazov, Anna Karenina, Madame Bovary,* or of the sleeping-bag scene in *For Whom the Bell Tolls*.

Authors have two choices in writing about sex: write with restraint, without spelling it out, or write explicit sex *providing there is a purpose beyond the simple act itself.* John Braine in *Room at the Top* (London: Methuen, 1957) gives a fine example of the former:

> We were out in the streets with our arms around each other's waists and turning in and out of narrow alleys and streets and courts and patches of waste ground and over a footbridge with engines clanging together aimlessly in the cold below ... and then we were in a corner of a woodyard in a little cave of piled timber; I took my hand away from her body, which performed all the actions she expected of it. She clung to it after the scalding, trembling moment of fusion as if it were human, kissing its drunken face....

I was surprised to read that section because I read the book *after* I had seen the movie, and there was some dialogue in the movie for which Braine can claim no credit. They were written by the scriptwriter Neal Patterson. In the movie, after Laurence Harvey and Heather Sears have left the woodyard hand in hand, Heather-Mavis, excited, having lost her virginity, asks, "Joe, did I make love well?" Laurence Harvey, indifferently looking in the other direction, says in a thick Lancashire accent, "Mavis, you make love the way you play tennis."

In my novel *Marpessa* (called *Sweet Marpessa* in an earlier edition) I have one explicit sex scene in which Marpessa, Marchioness of Glastonbury, comprehensively seduces a twelve-year-old schoolboy. The seduction is described in detail. What I was seeking to convey was not the venality of the British aristocracy, but its vulnerability and how, in Marpessa's case, it was leading her to her own destruction. If I did my job properly, the reader would not be getting whatever titillation was aroused by the sex act with the boy, but rather the fear of the doom which Marpessa was preparing for herself.

Sex can succeed in your novel if you see it in terms of contrast and conflict. The conflict could be class conflict or age conflict or even sexual conflict. The real shock of *Lady Chatterley's Lover* when it was first published was not so much the sex, but that Lady Chatterley was having sex with her husband's gamekeeper. In *Room at the Top,* Joe the working lad is having sex with the boss's daughter. In *Marpessa,* the participants were a thirty-five-year-old titled woman and a twelve-year-old boy.

Those are the conflicts of class and of age. To try to make a conflict of sex itself is the trap into which many a novelist has fallen. A Pennsylvania steelworker having sex with a McDonald's waitress or an Ivy League boy having sex with a Bryn Mawr girl presents no intrinsic conflict to the reader. They are doing what is expected of them. But if the working-class girl is aspiring to something higher in life—an education and a career—and is raped and thus soiled by a boy from her own gutter-ghetto class; if the Bryn Mawr sexpot deliberately imposes herself on an Ivy League boy she suspects to be homosexual, the necessary conflict is there.

More than anything else in the writing of fiction, more than dialogue, more than characterization, describing the sex act is an acquired art. It may be the most professional trick in all fiction writing. Fiction readers can forgive bad dialogue. If they didn't, no one would read Agatha Christie or Harold Robbins. They can forgive feeble characterization: many of Dickens' characters are so banal as to be unreadable. But a writer cannot get by with a sex scene that the reader senses as wrong, coarse, tasteless, uninformed, and *above all* unnecessary. It becomes an insult to the reader's intelligence and he, or more likely she, closes the book.

There should almost never be an explicit sex scene between husband and wife, because it involves no conflict whatever. That is what they married for. In fact, a sex scene involving a married couple could be more offensive to the reader than anything else. It could be considered a kind of invasion of sanctified privacy.

If the writer needs to explain the marital relationship in sexual terms, he should get it over and done with: "After fifteen years of marriage, Bill and Mary were still ardent lovers," and leave it at that. The reader will know all that is necessary to know.

I said that there should *almost* never be a sex scene between husband and wife. The caveat does not apply when there is passionate or furious conflict in the marriage. Here are two examples. Vanessa hates her husband, Clive. Clive is sexually insatiable, so every sex act is a rape of Vanessa. Or Clive hates Vanessa. She knows it and enjoys it. She has the money. She humiliates him by forcing him into sex that is repugnant to him. This is one of the themes of Sidney Sheldon's *Bloodline*.

Sex writing has its fundamental formulae and words, like the formulae and words of organized sport; the fascination with a woman's breasts, nipples, male power or its absence, bare bodies, thighs, orgasms, detumescence, fellatio, pain, delight, tears, post-coital laughter, indoor, outdoor. Make it as vivid as you feel and as explicit as you want, but don't struggle; don't try to write anything you feel in your heart you can't do; don't force your writing because you have been told that "sex sells." The result will be the same as watching a novice stripper doing her act: mutual embarrassment all around.

A strange parenthesis is intruding here. I find that I am instinctively addressing myself to a male writer. My experience has been that when we are dealing with sex writing, female writers tend to be more relaxed, more flexible, imaginative, and *dé-*

contracté than male writers. Female writers are more *interested* in sex scenes and more open to innovation. I have found this out both as author—from the reactions I have received—and as a professor—from the manuscripts I have read. Sex in fiction tends to give a woman the freedom to fantasize. Men are more likely to prefer the specifics of sex in erotic photography, X-rated movies, flesh magazines, or the sight of girls on stage. A woman I know loved *The History of* O by Pauline Réage, the strange novel of feminine sexual subjugation and torture. But she showed no interest in an illustrated edition that was published a few years ago by Grove Press.

Yet women writers are less surefooted when writing of obscenities and usually avoid them. In my opinion, rightly so. The less, the better. Like sex, obscenities should be used for a purpose. Before you start using the inevitable f——and sh——, think. Or, at any rate, plan. Use it as your ace in the hole. If your truck driver character casually says "f——" in a coffee shop off an interstate highway, he is contributing absolutely nothing to the edification of the reader. The language is expected of him. Truck drivers talk like that. If your kids in an inner-city school pour out torrents of obscenities that you faithfully record in your novel, the same sense of emptiness applies. So what, says the reader.

But if the vicar's wife rips her dress and thinking she is alone exclaims, "Oh, f——" into an open intercom and is heard by the congregation seated in church, we are getting somewhere!

On page 18 of one of the editions of *Commander Amanda* (New York: Zebra Books, 1976) Amanda is making a speech to local dignitaries. She is a member of Parliament, war hero, loving daughter of a bishop, and almost unbearably virtuous—or so the reader thinks so far.

> She turned with poise to her distinguished neighbors at the table of honor. A smile, deprecatory to the French ambassador and the minister. To her husband, his hands clapping upward toward her face, a friendlier smile, more intimate. To her father, the bishop of East Anglia, a different smile, respectful but loving. He was a man

> of such probity that she was sure if he ever committed even the tiniest sin, or had even a slightly improper thought, he would arraign himself before the tribunal of his own conscience for shriving. She knew every thought in the dear old man's head. To her younger sister Jennifer, Amanda had a different smile still, a warm, huggy big-sister smile. Amanda noted that the raving little nymphomaniac had left her husband behind, baby-sitting, which meant that she would stop on the way home and get f—— by the municipal gardener....

That last sentence, coming after such a deluge of smugness, primness, and self-righteousness is meant to act like a tweak on the nose, confronting the reader with the last word in the English language he expects to see. And although there is spoof-sex galore to come, the word is never repeated, nor is any other obscenity used in the book.

So your best service to yourself and your reader is to censor yourself. Ask yourself if your sex and your obscenities truly contribute to the narrative and the plot, and if you decide yes, plunge in at the deep end. But remember also that the tousled young man sitting on the edge of the unmade bed in the cold morning light, reaching down and picking up a bobby pin from the carpet leaves us in little doubt about what went on the night before.

Now we return to the subject of dialogue. Of all aspects of novel writing, none plays a greater con job on the reader than dialogue. The art of dialogue lies in leading the reader to think that the characters are speaking as they do in everyday life, when they are doing nothing of the sort. What people speak in normal life is conversation, not dialogue. Conversation is exchange of information: "What's the time?" "Six o'clock." That's conversation, but it is not dialogue. Think what happens when you pick up a telephone and find yourself on a crossed line. You listen in at first silently, intrigued at being a party to the unconscious intimacy of strangers. But you soon lose interest in exchanges such as:

"What are you doing?"

"Nothing much. I'm off to the launderette."

"Are you seeing Frank tonight?"

"I don't know. Maybe."

"Is he still at the same job?"

"Oh, yes. He likes it."

You hang up. It is empty, slow, repetitive, except to the two speakers themselves. This is the way we all speak more often than not, but it is not dialogue.

Conversation drifts along from thought to thought. It lacks the hard precise objective of a last chapter which tells it all and sums it all up. That is the aim of dialogue, to get there. Dialogue is a matter of *economy* and *direction*. In a novel every sentence, every line of dialogue, every *silence* is advancing the story by that much. No sentence should be quite what the reader is expecting to read, but the dialogue should be sufficiently close to life that he can actually believe he is reading words the way people use them in real life.

Take our adventure with the crossed telephone line, and let's see what would make it worthwhile to continue to listen in, to advance our understanding of the two:

"What are you doing?"

"The launderette calls. Why is it that my purse is always overloaded with quarters and dimes except on the morning I have to do the wash?"

"Are you seeing Frank tonight?"

"Ask Frank."

"Is anything wrong? Is he at the same job?"

"Is he! The job's a damn body-snatcher. If I see the walking zombie tonight, I'll tell him, 'Frank, it's the job or me.'"

In this version, you will note there is not a single direct reply on either side.

The secret of controlling dialogue rests on two words, *response* and *indirectness.* I used the word direction before. That is not to be confused with directness or indirectness.

Response first: What is *stated* is unimportant. The essence of dialogue is the *reply.* Let us take as humdrum a statement as I can think of:

"It's still raining."

There is nothing wrong with that as a statement to start off a dialogue. But a response like "I know" or "So what else is new?" or "It never seems to stop" are unacceptable. But how about, "According to the radio, if it keeps on for another twenty-four hours, we are going to make the Guinness *Book of Records."* That response has a certain twist that lifts it out of the commonplace, yet stays within the confines of credibility.

Oscar Wilde was the master of response, and I will give you a test in Wilde's art. Wilde encountered Frank Harris, author of *My Life and Loves* and an engaging scoundrel who stalked London literary society at the turn of the century. Harris said, "Oscar, I have been invited to every great house in London."

Determine for yourself what response you would have made to that. "Come off it." "Perhaps that is where we met?" "Did you leave any silverware behind?"

What Oscar Wilde actually said in response was, "More than once, Frank?"

Another example of unimportant statement and stimulating response: "What do you want for breakfast?" The unacceptable reply is "bacon and eggs." Forget it and think of the infinity of acceptable responses. If you want to be jocular or pretentious: "A loaf of bread, a flask of wine, and thou beside me sitting in the wilderness, but I'll settle for bacon and eggs." Or, "I know what I want first. I'll have bacon and eggs afterwards."

You may laugh, but briefly and more vividly than any narrative, you have conveyed love, affection, rapport, a mutual happiness. If you will pardon a mixed metaphor, you have created your image with a brushstroke of dialogue. Here is Anthony Powell in "A Buyer's Market," from *A Dance to the Music of Time* (Boston: Little, Brown) describing a pompous man without a scintilla of humor but with a huge ego. All is dialogue. There is not a word of description:

> 'As a matter of fact, I have been about very little this summer,' he said, frowning. 'I found I had been working a shade too hard, and had to—well—give myself a bit of a rest.... Then, the year before, I got jaundice in the middle of the season.'
>
> 'Are you fit again now?'
>
> I am better ... But I intend to take care of myself ... My mother often tells me I go at things too hard. Besides, I don't really get enough air and exercise—without which one can never be truly robust.'
>
> 'Do you still go down to Barnes and drive golf-balls into a net?'
>
> 'Whenever feasible' ...
>
> 'Actually one can spend too much time on sport if one is really going to get on.... And then I have my Territorials.'
>
> 'You were going to be a solicitor when we last met.'
>
> 'That would hardly preclude me from holding a Territorial officer's commission....'
>
> 'Of course it wouldn't.'
>
> 'I am with a firm of solicitors—Turnbull, Welford and Puckering, to be exact,' he said. 'But you may be sure that I have other interests too. Some of them not unimportant, I might add.'

And here is James Joyce, in *Ulysses*, conveying intellectuality confronted with peasant simplicity through dialogue, without stating in any way that one person is an intellectual and the other person is a simple peasant:

> The blessings of God on you, Buck Milligan cried, jumping from his chair. Sit down. Pour out the tea there. The sugar is in the

bag. Here, I can't go fumbling at the damned eggs. He hacked through the fry on the dish and slapped it out on three plates, saying:

In nominee Patris et Filii et Spiritus Sancti.

Haines sat down to pour out the tea.

I'm giving you two lumps each, he said. But, I say, Mulligan, you do make strong tea, don't you?

Buck Mulligan, hewing thick slices from the loaf, said in an old woman's wheedling voice:

When I makes tea I makes tea, as old mother Grogan said. And when I makes water I makes water.

By Jove, it is tea, Haines said.

Buck Mulligan went on hewing and wheedling:

So I do, Mrs. Cahill, says she. Begob, ma'am, says Mrs. Cahill, God send you don't make them in the one pot....

The doorway was darkened by an entering form.

The milk, sir.

Come in, ma'am, Mulligan said. Kinch, get the jug. An old woman came forward and stood by Stephen's elbow.

That's a lovely morning, sir, she said. Glory be to God.

To whom? Mulligan said, glancing at her. Ah, to be sure.

Stephen reached back and took the milkjug from the locker.

The islanders, Mulligan said to Haines casually, speak frequently of the collector of prepuces.

How much, sir? asked the old woman.

A quart, Stephen said....

It is indeed, ma'am, Buck Mulligan said, pouring milk into their cups.

Taste it, sir, she said.

He drank at her bidding.

If we could only live on good food like that, he said to her somewhat loudly, we wouldn't have the country full of rotten teeth and rotten guts. Living in a bogswamp, eating cheap food and the streets paved with dust, horsedung and consumptives' spits.

Are you a medical student, sir? the old woman asked.

I am, ma'am, Buck Mulligan answered....

Do you understand what he says? Stephen asked her.

Is it French you are talking, sir? the old woman said to Haines.

Haines spoke to her again a longer speech, confidently.

Irish, Buck Mulligan said. Is there Gaelic on you?

I thought it was Irish, she said, by the sound of it. Are you from the west, sir?

I am an Englishman, Haines answered.

He's English, Buck Mulligan said, and he thinks we ought to speak Irish in Ireland.

Sure we ought to, the old woman said, and I'm ashamed I don't speak the language myself. I'm told it's a grand language by them that knows.

Grand is no name for it, said Buck Mulligan. Wonderful entirely. Fill us out some more tea, Kinch. Would you like a cup, ma'am?

What a vivid picture! You almost know that the kettle is boiling on an open fire, and that the old lady is wearing black.

On to indirectness, a subject I have not in fact left. By indirection I also mean the *non sequitur.* My dictionary defines the *non sequitur* as "It does not follow; the derivation of a particular result which could not logically spring from a particular cause."

An example of indirection in dialogue:

"Do you agree with what I say?"

A direct reply would be no, and the result is aimless. A reply such as, "I doubt whether even *you* agree with what you say" jerks the reader forward.

I suspect your manuscript contains excellent indirect dialogue without your knowing it, if you are on your first novel. How to spot it is this. Dialogue is usually brief. Go over your manuscript and check whether you have a character speaking three sentences or more. Check the reply. You are likely to find that the response is also in three sentences or more. Break it up. Here is an example of how I restructured a student's dialogue without changing a word:

> Ignoring Jeanne, Wilbur said, "Thanks, Ralph. I was afraid to bring the subject up in front of Jeanne. She has her own views on politics, and I'm not her favorite candidate," he added, smiling.
>
> Jeanne replied, "You can speak to me directly if you wish. I know your views. If I can't change them, there's nothing I can do about it."
>
> "I'm not worried," Wilbur said. "So long as you can't vote here."

The sequence consists of three uninterrupted sentences, followed by three uninterrupted sentences, followed by two uninterrupted sentences. Note how much more forcefully the sequence reads when it is broken up:

> Ignoring Jeanne, Wilbur said, "Thanks, Ralph. I was afraid to bring the subject up in front of Jeanne."
>
> Jeanne replied, "You can speak to me directly if you wish."
>
> "She has her own views on politics, and I'm not her favorite candidate," said Wilbur, continuing to ignore her.
>
> "I know your views. If I can't change them, there's nothing I can do about it," Jeanne retorted.
>
> "I'm not worried," Wilbur said. "So long as you can't vote here."

The exchange now consists of two sentences, one sentence, one sentence, two sentences, two sentences.

There are so many masters of dialogue, from Oscar Wilde to Neil Simon and Woody Allen, that any quotation from me would be bound to be inadequate. Instead, I recently ran into some charmingly unexpected Edwardian dialogue in *Graustark*, written in 1903 by George Barr McCutcheon. Note the clever interplay, the sparring, the constant repetition of the slightly unexpected.

> "It depends on the"—he paused—"the princess, I should say."
>
> "Alas! There is one more fresh responsibility acquired. It seems to me that everything depends on the princess," she said, merrily.

"Not entirely," he said, quickly. "A great deal—a very great deal—depends on circumstances. For instance, when you were Miss Guggenslocker it wouldn't have been necessary for the man to be a prince, you know."

"But I was Miss Guggenslocker because a man was unnecessary," she said, so gravely that he smiled. "I was without a title because it was more womanly than to be a 'freak,' as I should have been had every man, woman and child looked upon me as a princess. I did not travel through your land for the purpose of exhibiting myself, but to learn and unlearn."

"I remember it cost you a certain coin to learn one thing," he observed.

"It was money well spent, as subsequent events have proved. I shall never regret the spending of that half gavvo. Was it not the means of bringing you to Edelweiss?"

"Well, it was largely responsible, but I am inclined to believe that a certain desire on my part would have found a way without the assistance of the coin. You don't know how persistent an American can be."

"Would you have persisted had you known I was a princess?" she asked.

"Well, I can hardly tell about that, but you must remember I didn't know who or what you were."

"Would you have come to Graustark had you known I was its princess?"

"I'll admit I came because you were Miss Guggenslocker."

"A mere woman."

"I will not consent to the word 'mere.' What would you think of a man who came half-way across the earth for the sake of a *mere* woman?"

"I should say he had a great deal of curiosity," she responded, coolly.

"And not much sense. There is but one woman a man would do so much for, and she could not be a *mere* woman in his eyes."

"If you were a novel writer, Mr. Lorry, what manner of heroine would you choose?" she asked, with a smile so tantalizing that he understood instinctively why she was reviving a topic once abandoned. His confusion was increased. Her uncle and aunt were regarding him calmly,—expectantly, he imagined.

"I—I have no ambition to be a novel writer," he said, "so I have not made a study of heroines."

"But you would have an ideal," she persisted.

"I'm sure I—I don't think—that is, she would not necessarily be a heroine. Unless, of course, it would require heroism to pose as an ideal for such a prosaic fellow as I."

"To begin with, you would call her Clarabel Montrose or something equally as impossible. You know the name of a heroine in a novel must be euphonious. That is an exacting rule." It was an open taunt, and he could see that she was enjoying his discomfiture. It aroused his indignation and his wits.

"I would first give my hero a distinguished name. No matter what the heroine's name might be—pretty or otherwise—I could easily change it to his in the last chapter."

At least half of all dialogue will be perfectly comprehensible without any attribution whatever, but when attribution must be given, the simplest and best verb is *said*, followed by *asked*. I don't say eliminate from your text, *he responded*, *she exclaimed*, *they cried*, *he retorted*—I have heard professors of creative writing offer such verbs as alternatives to *said* (being a guest I cringed and remained silent). But in probably ninety percent of dialogue, *he said* or *she said* is best. All other sentiments should be made clear by the dialogue itself.

A particular problem in dialogue is rendering accented and vernacular speech. As a general rule, avoid both, since neither are strictly necessary. Anthony Burgess uses vernacular in *Clockwork Orange*. D. H. Lawrence uses vernacular frequently, and he is a giant. So do minnows like Bram Stoker, in *Dracula*, but it remains a bloody awful practice. "Eet ees zo wondairfool to watch ze tennis," said Yvonne. "Wimbledon ees zo beautifool." This is ghastly. How about, "It is so wonderful to watch tennis," said Yvonne. 'Wimbledon is so beautiful.' Sebastian noticed that Yvonne gave 'Wimbledon' a French pronunciation but was too tactful to say so. She would learn."

The occasional repetition of "I declare" is usually ample to convey the South. A fellow addressed as "Cobber" can be presumed to be Australian. Where accent is more obscure but needs to be established, the author can introduce precise comment:

> "I am South African," said Joanna Jongbloed.
>
> "I know," he said.
>
> "How?"
>
> "By the way you say 'Sith Ifricin.'"

In *Giselle* (New York: Putnam, 1975) I introduce a precocious teenager called June, who describes *Swan Lake* to an amused company of her elders. Without resorting to a single Lisa-Doolittle-like "cor blimey," I think I conveyed clearly that she was a little Cockney kid.

> "It's all about this kinky prince who goes out with his courtiers to shoot some ducks and flips his biscuit over a swan called Odette, see? The reason he knows she's called Odette is because the Royal Swanners typed the name out on a Dymo and stuck it on her beak. But lo and behold, who should turn up but a Pakistani ponce swan called Robert*, who's got a kid sister called Odile. Robert sees that the prince, being a Pole, isn't too bright upstairs, so he substitutes Odile for Odette at a ball, figuring all swans look alike to the Poles. They dance. Then Odette bangs on the window of the Royal palace. The prince twigs, and, mad as hell, tears off one of the wings of the Pakistani ponce swan who flings round and round and round, and dies, circumscribed."

*Rothbart in the ballet.

There I think one gets a sense of both vernacular and accent without a word of either. I used another technique to convey important accent in *The Fourth Horseman*. Again it was done by *describing* accent rather than mimicking it. A band of Irish and English mercenaries are about to attack Hollywood Park racetrack. Chief of security at Hollypark is Jim McGrady, who is puzzled by the number of Irishmen turning up at the track. He confides his fears to his mistress:

> "It was not until after the second Irish visitation that I began to get disturbed and scratch my head. From then on I had photographs taken by hidden cameras. So far we have records of seven men and one woman. And more coming in."
>
> Doris rose and stretched and played with the strings at the throat of her peignoir. McGrady went on. "They all had one thing in common."
>
> "They were Irish."
>
> "More than that, Doris." McGrady bared his teeth as though he had had an attack of gas. "Doris, they were from Belfast. Or at least from Northern Ireland. Not from the Republic."
>
> Doris said, "I'm impressed, Jim. How could you tell?"
>
> "The Dublin accent is as different from the Belfast accent as Brooklyn is from Memphis. Dubliners speak softly, polysyllabically, and they like to use rich words. Belfast people are more staccato, harsher. They find it harder to get the words out, so they chew them first."

The message, I guess, is to eliminate the positive, and accentuate the negative. If you have a character from Brooklyn, you don't have him say in your dialogue expressions like "toidy-toid and toid." But you may file in your mind some such experience as I had once when arriving in New York aboard the Queen Mary. Unloading was even slower than usual and I asked a docker why. "You came in second. Foist we had to unload the LeeBOIT." He meant the Liberté. Not only was that taking Brooklynese to a pinnacle beyond which it can never rise, but it entitles me to carry the word "foist" up with it!

From dialogue and accent let's go on to an even more adventurous venture in the quicksands of monologue. Monologue is one of the most challenging forms of fiction to write and satisfying to read. But it has to *aspire* to literature, even if it falls short. Offered diffidently, it cannot win.

It is supereffective in connoting extreme emotion, madness, stress carried to the unbearable. Usually it involves a complete suspension of logic, but it is held together by a strange, almost subconscious, undercurrent of sense that keeps the reader straining to understand it. (For a masterpiece of lunatic-logical monologue read the speech of the slave in Samuel Beckett's *Waiting for Godot.*) Yet monologue can be used only sparingly, for it is too creamy rich for overindulgence.

I have used it twice in my dozen or so novels. Once was in a book called *Amanda in Spain*. Amanda has tracked down and captured a diabolical French priest wanted by the postwar French government for war crimes and the torture of Resistance fighters, including Amanda herself. For reasons of plot she releases him. She is at the wheel of a car at midnight, with Father Grotius and his younger brother, Sauveur, in the back seat:

> To Amanda Grotius said, "My brother and I are peasants and orphans. We grew up believing *Benedicta sit Mater Dei*. Are you so naive, Madame Amanda, or so bigoted, to think for one moment, from our birth to our present crisis, we have not questioned our calling? Have we not thought, discussed together, whether we might not have served our Lord better in the fields, or repairing motor cars, or working as electricians? I am a man of intense sexual lust. My younger brother is more pure. But how can my brother and myself, who speak no language other than our own, and the Latin of the village priests, our education limited by the seminary, compete with clever men like Nestorius saying such heresies—to us—as that Mary is not the Mother of God because she carried the Man and not the God in her womb at the miracle of the Incarnation? How does a simple peasant react when he engages in argument with such casuistry? The answer is, he doesn't. Defeated on every point of polemic he knocks the clever

man down with his fist. My brother and I answered the heresies of the Jews and freemasons with our fists and our swords, against satanics and goats ... I drew my sword for the Son and His Mother and they called me a war criminal. I raised the dead and they called me a devil. You people can't have it all ways. But you try. My word, how you try."

Amanda, overwhelmed by this torrent of argument of which she understood only a fraction, could only say, "What about Sauveur, your brother?"

Grotius turned in the confined space and hit the younger man with great force across the face. Sauveur flinched. "He is not wanted by the official bandits in France. He can go back to France tomorrow, but the fool babbles about following me into exile, abandoning God's work...."

"Not abandoning, Mayol" said Sauveur, holding his cheek. "That is not fair. I am not abandoning...."

Grotius said, "I came secretly on the suggestion of Mother Hildegarde whom I visited in the hospital of Corpus Christi. I did not know I was to meet the Nazi, Willi Schleger. He burned a village near ours in Tarn, rounded up old women whom I had confessed, little children I had baptized, locked them in the church and set fire to it.... I will hold my sword against the heretic's throat until he feels the divine impress, and repents. I hold it there while the blood drops, ruby by ruby, and he shrivels in fear...."

Amanda said, "... I came here to track you down and hand you over to the French ... I refuse to call you Father ... We finish up saving each other's lives. That does not in any way signify that I have forgiven you."

Grotius shouted, "Forgive! What is forgive! I abominate you, your country and your body ... But I am not sorry I encountered you again. I shall hound you and thrash you every time I come across you. Do me a favour. Read about the Virgin of Antipolo, Our Lady of Peace and Happy Voyage. After that you may change. If not, I hope to see you crumbled. Out Sauveur, you rascal."

Father Grotius and his brother were gone in a misty swirl of wintry wind, through the open door, black cowls and scapulars disappearing almost instantly into the starless night....

And do you know which I think is the most interesting sentence in the above? "You people can't have it all ways," a totally contemporary, everyday expression carrying its own sanity in the torrent of madness.

Remember that I am talking about monologue, not so-called *interior monlogue*. Monologue is *talk*. It is not the expression of inner thought. Ernest Hemingway's *Old Man and the Sea* was all inner thought, not monologue. On the other hand, *The Fall* by Albert Camus is monologue carried to the extent that one may mentally drop the quotes from the sentences and count it as narrative. Sherlock Holmes often uses almost clinical monologue in his brilliant deductions—those that are invariably followed by, "Amazing, my dear Holmes," and "Elementary, my dear Watson."

Two classic monologues of modern fiction come to my mind. One is at the end of *Death on the Installment Plan* by Louis-Ferdinand Céline, when Ferdinand's uncle, in seeking to divert the central character, Ferdinand, from committing suicide, stuns him and deafens him with a nonstop barrage of words. I will not quote it because of its obscenities. But I recommend the book to all who pursue creative writing. *Atlantic's Brief Lives* says of *Death on the Installment Plan (La Mort a Gage)*, written in 1936,

> Immediately acclaimed, this hallucinatory, autobiographical work, in seemingly crude, slangy style, expressing morbid despair and full of obscenities, crime and the dregs of humanity, is a precursor of black humor and the literature of the absurd. . . .

The other superb use of monologue appears toward the end of *Lolita* by Vladimir Nabokov. Humbert Humbert has tracked down Quilty, the man who stole his nymphet Lolita from him, and has a gun trained on him (Humbert Humbert does in fact shoot him dead after Quilty's desperate, brilliant, funny, horrifying plea for his life to be spared):

"Now look here, Mac," he said, "You are drunk and I am a sick man. Let us postpone the matter. I need quiet. I have to nurse my impotence. Friends are coming in the afternoon to take me to a game. This pistol-packing farce is becoming a frightful nuisance. We are men of the world, in everything—sex, free verse, marksmanship. If you bear me a grudge, I am ready to make unusual amends. Even an old-fashioned *rencontre*, sword or pistol, in Rio or elsewhere—is not excluded. My memory and my eloquence are not at their best today but really, my dear Mr. Humbert, you were not an ideal stepfather, and I did not force your little *protégée* to join me. It was she made me remove her to a happier home. This house is not as modern as that ranch we shared with dear friends. But it is roomy, cool in summer and winter, and in a word comfortable, so, since I intend retiring to England or Florence forever, I suggest you move in. It is yours, gratis. Under the condition you stop pointing at me that [he swore disgustingly] gun. By the way, I do not know if you care for the bizarre, but if you do, I can offer you, also gratis, as house pet, a rather exciting little freak, a young lady with three breasts, one a dandy, this is a rare and delightful marvel of nature. Now *soyons raisonables*. You will only wound me hideously and then rot in jail while I recuperate in a tropical setting. I promise you, Brewster, you will be happy here, with a magnificent cellar, and all the royalties from my next play—I have not much at the bank right now but I propose to borrow—you know, as the Bard said, with that cold in his head, to borrow and to borrow and to borrow. There are other advantages. We have here a most reliable and bribable charwoman, a Mrs. Vibrissa—curious name—who comes from the village twice a week, alas not today, she has daughters, granddaughters, a thing or two I know about the chief of police makes him my slave. I am a playwright. I have been called the American Maeterlinck. Maeterlinck-Schmetterling, says I. Come on! All this is very humiliating, and I am not sure I am doing the right thing. Never use herculanita with rum. Now drop that pistol like a good fellow. I knew your dear wife slightly. You may use my wardrobe. Oh, another thing—you are going to like this. I have an absolutely unique collection of erotica upstairs. Just to mention one item: the in folio de-luxe *Bagration Island* by the explorer and psychoanalyst Melanie Weiss, a remarkable lady, a remarkable work—drop that gun—with photographs of eight hundred and something male organs she examined and measured in 1932 on Bagration, in the Barda Sea, very illuminating graphs, plotted with love under pleasant skies—drop that gun—and moreover I can arrange for you to attend executions, not everybody knows that the chair is painted yellow—"

The fact that all three of these examples of monologue come at the end of the book is significant. (Beckett's does not, but the slave's monologue is startling in a different context.) Monologue is almost invariably climactic, often so much so that it can be reserved only for the final climax. The writer must study it with care before he writes it. I suggest you prepare for it in advance, jotting down any strange or errant thought that comes to mind and then assembling it into a whole. Concentrate on the nonsense first, the fantasy, the funny one-liner, the unconnected thought. The sense will come later and provide the cement that will hold the verbal Tower of Babel together.

If, in this chapter, I have made dialogue sound like one of the most difficult aspects of the narrative writer's craft, I'm sorry, but it is. Fortunately, like so much else, it yields to practice. So be of good cheer and be resolute. And bear in mind some of the hints I have given you. They may not help you much at first, but as you become more proficient, they will speed you on your way.

7

PUTTING IT ALL TOGETHER

No matter how good you are at action or characterization or description, in the end you still will have to blend them together so naturally that they always will complement—and never detract from—one another.

No single rule will tell you how to do this except, perhaps, the rule that says that whenever you begin to sense that you may be going on too long in any particular vein, you are!

Striking the right balance is essential, and nowhere more than in beginnings and endings. I know one busy editor who says that whenever he hasn't the time to do a thorough job of line editing a manuscript (line editing, incidentally, is not the same thing as copy editing; it is a much more creative function, closer to the writing process itself), he nevertheless insists on carefully line editing the first forty pages, then the concluding two pages of each chapter, and the last fifteen pages of the manuscript. He says that this will give him about a seventy-five percent chance of finding the most serious, and more easily rectifiable, errors. If you can do your own line editing following these principles, you will have a more saleable novel to present to a publisher.

The good editor is nearly always right. The way a novel begins may color the reader's attitude toward the rest of the book.

In fact, it may persuade him that there's not going to be any rest-of-the-book. Proust's *A la Recherche due Temps Perdu* nearly foundered at birth while publishers struggled through the apparently endless opening, and many who claim to adore Vladimir Nabokov's *Ada* never made it past those first three prickly chapters.

A friend said of one of the novels of John Buchan, "It improves after the fourth chapter."

To which another replied, "Yes, but who knows that except John?"

Publishers and authors have long believed that novels have to begin with a high-powered action scene—the so-called "hook"—violent, provocative, mysterious, shocking, and the more so the better. Somerset Maugham put it at its simplest. He wrote that it is often wise for an author to let the reader know "what he is in for." Although most Victorian novelists began with leisurely descriptive passages, many were just as aware of a fast start as novelists are today. No one wrote a faster start than Herman Melville in *Moby Dick*, published in 1851:

> "Call me Ishmael."

H. Rider Haggard wrote *King Solomon's Mines* in 1885. After an introductory first paragraph, he began his second with a touch of provocation that gives the reader delicious warning of a book not to be put down until finished:

> I am laid up here in Durban with the pain and trouble in my left leg. Ever since that confounded lion got hold of me I have been liable to it.

Charles Dickens was always, or nearly always, aware of the value of a strong start. The swinging rhetoric of his first paragraph in *A Tale of Two Cities*:

> It was the best of times. It was the worst of times, it was the age of foolishness, it was the epoch of belief, it was the epoch of

incredulity, it was the season of light, it was the spring of hope, it was the winter of despair.

Bleak House may have been Dickens' dullest novel, but you would never guess it by the first paragraph:

LONDON. Michaelmas Term lately over, and the Lord Chancellor sitting in Lincoln's Inn Hall. Implacable November weather. As much mud in the streets, as if the waters had but newly retired from the face of the earth, and it would not be wonderful to meet a Megalosoraus, forty feet or so long, waddling like an elephantine lizard up Holborn Hill. Smoke lowering down from chimney-pots making a soft black drizzle, with flakes of soot in it as big as full-grown snow-flakes ... dogs indistinguishable in mire. Horses, scarcely better; splashed to their very blinkers. Foot passengers, jostling one another's umbrellas in a general infection of ill-temper, and losing their foothold at street corners, where tens of thousands of other foot-passengers have been slipping and sliding since the day broke (if this day ever broke), adding new deposits to the crust upon crust of mud, sticking at those points to the pavement and accumulating compound interest.

Fog everywhere. Fog up the river, where it flows among green aits and meadows; fog down the river where it rolls defiled among the tiers of shipping, and the waterside pollutions of a great (and dirty) city.

And so it goes on, Dickens piling image upon image until half way down the second page—with the following example of how a master of the English language writes:

Never can there come fog too thick, never can there come mud and mire too deep, to assort with the groping and floundering condition which this High Court of Chancery, most pestilent of hoary sinners, holds this day, in the sight of heaven and earth.

Trent's Last Case, by E. C. Bentley, was written in 1913. It is still one of the detective novels most highly praised by writers of detective novels, among them Agatha Christie, Dorothy L.

Sayers, Freeman Crofts, J. S. Fletcher, and Edgar Wallace. Consider the vivid summary opening:

> When the scheming, indomitable brain of Sigsbee Manderson was shattered by a shot from an unknown hand, that world lost nothing worth a single tear; it gained something memorable in a harsh reminder of the vanity of such wealth as this dead man had piled up—without making one loyal friend to mourn him, without doing an act that could help his memory to the least honor. But when the news of his end came, it seemed to those living in the great vortices of business as if the earth too shuddered under the blow....
>
> A sharp spasm convulsed the convalescent sharelist. In five minutes the dull noise of the kerbstone market in Broad Street had leapt to a high note of frantic interrogation. From within the hive of the Exchange itself could be heard a droning hubbub of fear, and men rushed hatless in and out....

Dick Francis, excellent writer of racetrack thrillers, begins *Risk* (New York: Harper & Row, 1978) with a one-line trope:

> Thursday, March 17, I spent the morning in anxiety, the afternoon in ecstasy, and the evening unconscious.

Alexander Solzhenitsyn begins *Lenin in Zurich* at hurricane pace with a monologue:

> Yes, yes, yes, yes! It's a vice, this habit of plunging recklessly, of rushing full steam ahead intent only on your goal, blind and deaf to all around, so that you fail to see the childishly obvious danger beside you....

The fantasist novelist Alfred Bester begins his novella *Starlight* with a characterization:

> Take two parts of Beelzebub, two of Israel, one of Monte Cristo, one of Cyrano, mix violently, season with mystery and you have

> Mr. Solon Aquila. He is tall, gaunt, sprightly in manner, bitter in expression, and when he laughs his dark eyes turn into wounds. His occupation is unknown. He is wealthy without visible means of support. He is seen everywhere and known nowhere. There is something odd about him.

That brilliant but ultimately disappointing writer Françoise Sagan opens the first page of *Aimez Vous Brahms* with a somewhat different form of characterization:

> Paule gazed at her face in the mirror and studied the accumulated defeats of thirty-nine years, one by one, not with the panic—the resentment—usual at such times but with a detached calm. As though the warm skin, which her two fingers plucked now and then to accentuate a wrinkle or bring out a shadow, had belonged to someone else, to another Paule passionately concerned with her beauty and battling with the transition from young to not so young woman: a woman she scarcely recognized. She had stationed herself at the mirror to kill time, only to discover—she smiled at the thought—that time was gradually, painlessly killing her, aiming its blows at an appearance she knew had been loved.

Fine writing. The first paragraph of the book makes us know Paule intimately: her age, her beauty, her fear, her tactility. We cannot wait, yet we fear, to know more. Sagan's start is diamantine and coherent. But she is deliberately holding back. She has already convinced the reader that she is holding her horse for the second bend and advising us not to tear up our parimutuel slip yet.

Not so Judith Krantz, whose filly *Scruples* streaks out of the gate already two lengths ahead of the rest of the field.

> Billy Ikehorn Orsini—whose faults do not normally include a tendency to erratic driving—brought her vintage Bentley to a stop with an impatient screech in front of Scruples, the world's most lavish specialty store, a virtual club for the floating principality of the very, very rich and the truly famous. She was thirty-five, sole

mistress of a fortune estimated at between two hundred and two hundred fifty million dollars by the list-makers of the *Wall Street Journal.* Almost half of her wealth was tidily invested in tax-free municipal bonds, a simplification little appreciated by the IRS.

What this passage tells us is that Miss Krantz may not be much of a stylist, but she certainly knows how to get a story off the ground.

The openings I have quoted here do more than just arrest our attention. Some introduce us to central characters or essential settings, others give us hints as to what the theme or plot will be, some establish a mood, most convey an idea of the author's attitude toward his subject. It is not enough for an opening merely to arrest; it must be part of the story, even where it is flashback or prolepsis. Not only that, it must never be so strong that it overshadows subsequent climaxes: in storytelling or drama, what could be worse than beginning with an act that's impossible to follow? It can be done. Wren did it in *Beau Geste* with his opening fort of dead legionnaires at their embrasures, but that may have been beginner's luck. He never wrote as good a book again.

Thus the opening is, par excellence, the one point in the story where the writer must know what he is doing. Probably you will rewrite no other part of your manuscript so many times. But as my editor friend suggested, there are other points in the manuscript to watch.

Chapter endings are tricky, because they usually try to do two apparently contradictory things at once. Chapters are logically grouped conjuries of narrated events and information that form the building blocks of the story. As such, they have a tendency to be somewhat self-contained, and novelists are often tempted to round them off with neat little conclusions so as to bring them to a graceful end. But even a little of this can go a long way toward interfering with the forward momentum of the overall story. After all, it is not until the last page that we want the reader to close the book.

To that end, the author should in most instances end a chapter *interrogatively.* I italicize the word because I am not sure it is the right one. The French have an expression *laisser le faim sur le plat*, meaning that one leaves the table hungry for more.

Frequently I have read, both in manuscript and in published novels, a chapter ending something like this:

> Christine said goodnight, the touch of Michael's kiss still on her lips. She ran upstairs humming the tune to which they had been dancing, undressed, and sank into a deep, happy, and dreamless sleep.

Such an ending is final. It completes the cycle of events. It is not necessarily a bad ending, *providing* it follows a chapter so full of action that the reader is emotionally drained and needs a moment of peace. But my guess is that such an ending has not concluded that sort of chapter. I leave you with a test as to how to make it an ending that will lure the reader to keep reading. Here are a couple of thoughts:

> .... undressed and sank into a deep, happy, and dreamless sleep, a sleep so deep she was unaware of the bedroom door opening and the light in the hall gleaming on the switchblade held in a gloved hand.

> .... undressed and sank into a deep, happy, and dreamless sleep. Outside, Michael slid into the passenger seat of a waiting Ford Mustang, its windshield wipers clicking in the cold rain. "It worked like a charm," he said, patting the thigh of the woman in the driver's seat. "Tomorrow that pretty little girl will present me with a check for five hundred grand."

If you find on rereading your manuscript that you have been ending your chapters on a note of downbeat finality, there is an interesting rule of thumb by which you can correct it. At some place in the middle of the chapter you will find a dramatic moment of tension. (If you don't, you should be writing a different novel.) Find that dramatic moment of tension, end the chapter there, and almost invariably you will find that the next sentence makes an excellent start to the next chapter.

I checked a few specimen chapter endings written by America's top-selling novelists. Here is Ken Follett in *The Eye of the Needle* (New York: Arbor House, 1978):

> As he spoke, he tossed the lighted cigarette at Faber's face and reached for the gun above the windshield.
>
> The late hour had got to all of them. Bloggs's sudden excess of energy jerked them out of a creeping lethargy. One leaned forward, rubbing his hands; another tied his shoelaces; a third put his jacket on. They wanted to go to work. There were no comments, no questions.

And here is Robert Ludlum in *The Bourne Identity* (New York: Richard Marek Publishers, 1980). Ludlum is a master of the slightly downbeat tension of chapter endings. His last sentence quietly caps the key sentence that is his penultimate sentence, the last sentence but one:

> "Finally I want our team to take rooms within a block of the bank on the rue Madeleine. This time the bank will be Cain's undoing.... A bargain price as despicable as he is ... unless he's something else."
>
> "I'm going to talk to a man I think I knew. If he's got a brain in his head he'll listen. He's marked for extinction."

Sidney Sheldon in *Rage of Angels* (New York: William Morrow, 1980):

> Michael said slowly, "Nothing. Because that's not where Adam Warner is going to die."
>
> Mrs. Cooper shook her head.... She leaned forward, took Jennifer's hands in hers and dropped her voice to a whisper. "I'm going to give you Wyoming."

The best chapter ending I ever wrote to a novel, or at least the chapter ending that gave me the most pleasure, was in *Amanda's Castle*, set in Nazi Germany at the very end of the war, with the Russians encircling Berlin and the Americans and British across the Rhine. I was aided by my personal experience of time and place as a young war correspondent in World War II. Amanda Nightingale is shot down, in full uniform of the Women's RAF. Although there is almost nothing left of Hitler's Germany, she finds herself at a sinister castle full of prominent collaborators of the Germans. Many of the characters are identifiable for a roman à clef: Lord Haw Haw; General Vlasov, commander of the Russian Army that fought alongside the Wehrmacht against Stalin; Serge Lifar, the ballet dancer; Corinne Luchaire, the pre-World War II French movie star.

Amanda knocks on the door and is admitted by an old retainer in velvet knee breeches and satin stockings. Amanda feels like Alice in Wonderland, alone in the enemy's land, as yet still uncaptured. Incredibly, she finds herself at an enormous cocktail party, with everyone in evening dress:

> The sudden silence was total except for the sound of distant artillery. Amanda spoke at last. "What is this place, and who is in charge here?" she asked in English, in a loud, clear voice.... There was a hum of frightened talk, much of it uncomprehending and asking translation, and everybody looked in different directions as though the words had been issued from some hidden loudspeaker, or been uttered by a master ventriloquist. After several seconds, reluctantly, a tiny, elderly woman, in profound mourning black, edged to the front, assisted gently, with touches on the elbows, by the others. Her hair was white, but her aristocratic, still-unlined face must have been exceedingly beautiful once, and the country air in which she lived gave a lively, healthy touch to her pronounced cheekbones.... She spoke in accented English in a voice she strove to keep calm, and Amanda found herself, despite her own terror, respecting the woman's courage. "Are you American?" she asked. "Have the Allies

arrived? This is the Schloss Augsberg. My name is Dagmar, the baroness Feldstegen. You must forgive me, because I suffer greatly from neuralgia. . . . Are we now your prisoners?"

Amanda removed her gloves. "No, Baroness Feldstegen," she said, "I am yours."

As I have said, the only place where a real honest-to-goodness conclusion always is wanted is at the book's end. Even here one has to use care. In dramatic terms, the real conclusion comes in the final climactic scene, not in the formal conclusion that ends the book. It is practically impossible to construct a final climactic scene that will not only resolve the protagonist's conflict but simultaneously tie up all the loose ends developed during the course of the story's telling. Thus, the formal conclusion is normally a kind of anticlimax that follows the last big scene and tries, as quickly and effectively as possible, to deal with all remaining unanswered questions. If there are a lot of such questions, writing the formal conclusion can be a real chore. The conclusion must be brief enough so as not to detract from the final big scene's dramatic effect, yet it should not be so densely packed with last-minute information that it is awkward and tiresome to read. The only way around this dilemma is preplanning. You should try to tie up as many loose ends as possible *before* the climactic final scene, so that you leave youself a little elbow room when you come to the formal conclusion. In the space thus saved you can devote yourself to confecting some of those little grace notes—a final surprising twist in the story, a touch of rhetoric, an intriguing hint of things to come, a bright sliver of dialogue, or any of a host of other devices that can bring your novel to a satisfying, and perhaps even memorable, end.

8

SOME THOUGHTS ON STYLE

Writing at high speed is usually a good thing. It suggests enthusiasm, confidence, and knowing what you want to say. Don't hesitate to let yourself get carried away, but be careful later on to bring yourself back to earth. Among the literary debris left behind by writing up a storm are clichés, sloppy constructions, jargon, vogue words, and purple prose—the kind of embarrassing passages that achieve dubious immortality in those little inserts at the foot of the columns of *The New Yorker*: "Our Forgetful Authors," "In Love with Own Words Dept."

In Chapter 2 I quoted George Orwell's advice on the virtues of brevity in literary style. Use adverbs sparingly: actions and dialogue should speak for themselves. I think it was Mark Twain who said, "When you find an adverb, tread on it."

Watch for certain debilitating words like *because* and *when*.

If you start a sentence with any -ing, such as "Sitting on the sofa, she. . . ." or "Leaving the house, he. . . ." you have probably written a sloppy sentence.

Another danger word is *as*. I have noticed a funny thing about the word *as* when it appears in the middle of a sentence. It invariably separates two themes, the theme in the second part of the sentence being always the stronger of the two. When the *as* is removed the sentence is converted into two sentences and reversed, the impact is always stronger. Examples:

> *Weak:* Can't they see how lonely I am, Christine wondered as the conversation turned away from her to people and events about which she knew nothing.
>
> *Strong:* The conversation turned away from her and drifted to people and events about which she knew nothing. Can't they see how lonely I am, Christine wondered.
>
> *Weak:* The blue bottle slipped from her hand as she went down, skirt twisting above her thighs.
>
> *Strong:* She went down, skirt twisting above her thighs. The blue bottle slipped from her hand.
>
> *Weak:* She answered between laughs as she jumped over the rows of corn he had just planted.
>
> *Stronger:* She jumped over the rows of corn he had just planted and answered between laughs.

It is a fault committed by even the best of storytellers. Here is Sidney Sheldon in *Bloodline*, "'They really do you proud here,' John Swinton said, his mouth full as he chewed the remains of a large veal chop on his plate."

How much stronger it could have been: John Swinton, his mouth full, chewed the remains of a large veal chop on his plate. "They really do you proud here," he said.

Another fault common to almost all of us until it is caught and eliminated is what, for want of any other expression I know, I will call the "double positive." This consists of saying the same thing twice in different words. Example: "I know it's true," he said. "I'm convinced of it."

The temptation is obvious. We feel that the repetition doubles the emphasis. And in fact it is both valid and effective in other forms of writing, in theatrical dialogue or a screenplay. But we are writing a novel, and in fiction the double positive has an emasculating effect. Here is a quadruple example from a manuscript I read recently:

The mother is the power in that family. Her boys do exactly what she says. I don't know what else to say. There is nothing more I can tell you.

Four sentences doing the job that could be done by two. Mind you, nothing is absolute, and written sparingly, the double positive can be effective. But I have noticed that authors who use it once tend to repeat it to tedium.

Another source of tedium is perfunctory language. Everyday speech is filled with commonplace ways of saying commonplace things. This may be a convenient kind of shorthand in conversation, but, some classes of dialogue apart, it should be avoided in written prose. Interviewed by a newspaperwoman some time ago, I learned from her article that my accent was "unmistakably English." If it had been *affectedly English* or *stage English* or *BBC English*, I would have known that she had put a certain amount of care into her choice of words. But "unmistakably English" simply fell glib onto the type—without any application of thought. Beware the easy words, the lazy expressions that come from haste, in a brain gone stale. "Unmistakably English" is one in a vast army of trite literary automate increasingly thrown up by the communications explosion.

It is all to easy to make a collection of your own examples of unthinking thought. *Misguided conception*, *lavishly illustrated*, *plentiful supply*, *fevered imagination*, *conspicuous absence*, *significant contribution*, *gracious living*, *past history*, *enviable reputation*, *unenviable reputation*. One could compile a dictionary.

Villains and murderers of the English language lurk all around us—on television, Madison Avenue, the Nuclear Establishment, the Pentagon, the White House, the university campuses. Speechwriters will think up a snappy phrase or a buzzword like *buzzword*, and they and their imitators will use it to death. The Richard Nixon administration was particularly fruitful in its production of shoddy English. One recalls Ron Ziegler, President

Nixon's press secretary, recanting earlier untrue statements on Watergate by stating that what he had said before was "inoperative." "At this moment in time," in which Haldeman, Ehrlichman, Dean, and the rest seem forever suspended, may one day be the title for a new book on Watergate. *Gameplan, scenario, hanging tough, letting it all hang out* became senile before they had a chance to enjoy their youth. In fairness, Ehrlichman's conception of John Mitchell's "twisting slowly in the wind," presumably on a hook, gave a macabre indication of what Ehrlichman later showed—that he is a good writer.

The trouble about vogue expressions is not that they are wrong in themselves. On the contrary, they are often very good. The trouble is that they are overused. I once liked the word thrust as a noun, in the sense of *intention* or *purpose.* I thought the expression *bottom line,* meaning the final accounting or ultimate meaning, was sharp and vivid. Today they hit my nerve ends like water torture. So do *ball in your court* and *that's what it's all about.*

Collective wisdom and *educated guess* have a fine sonorous ring to them. But not after they have bounced a hundred times from the column of James Reston to the column of Anthony Lewis and into the mouths of Brinkley and Cronkite.

To aid one of my students in her novel, I composed a limerick for one of her characters. She said, "I had forgotten you are into limericks."

"I am not *into* limericks, Betty," I said. "You are not *into* limericks. Nobody in my class is *into* anything."

Some expressions hold their value. I like *spinoff.* I don't know who invented the word *gridlock* to describe the ultimate irreversible in traffic jams, but it says exactly what it means.

I may be laboring the point, but the use of prematurely redundant words and expressions poses a special hazard for the novelist. The progress of his work from writing to publishing is so slow. An expression that goes red hot onto his typewriter may be cold and stale two years later when his book comes out. The moral is, if you want to use a sharp and vivid expression, invent your own.

And when you do use an expression that you have thought about and decided was good, use it sparingly, probably not more than once in the entire book.

If Americans' capacity to invent telling new ways of expressing things is a tribute to their imagination, I am afraid their capacity to tolerate verbosity is not. There must be more than one explanation as to why verbosity is more an American than a British literary problem. Perhaps it stems in part from the size of the country, the huge spaces between communities, the early American necessity for oral tradition, and the taste for the telling of tall stories.

I will give examples of verbosity, because over the years I have found that Americans are as inured to verbosity as Soviet citizens are inured to the propaganda blaring from loudspeakers at every street corner. They do not hear it anymore than Americans see it.

There are signs in post offices that say "No Dogs Allowed," which alone is OK, even though post offices offer perhaps less temptation for a pup to blot its copybook than any other establishment, except perhaps an income tax office. But the post office sign writer adds "Except Seeing-Eye Dogs." First, neither the seeing-eye dog nor its master are likely to read the fine print. Furthermore, it is inconceivable that even the most sadistic postmaster would eject a blind man and his dog from his fief.

But the sign writer was still worried, and spotted a fatal flaw. The sign as it stands opens the post office to scores of cats, rabbits, budgerigars, hamsters and shoulderloads of pet monkeys. So to close the loophole, he finally added "No Pets Allowed."

It often seems to me that Americans rush into print for any or no reason. Every restaurant displays a prominent notice, "Occupancy by more than X people is dangerous and unlawful." How long is it, I wonder, since a law enforcement officer came to count heads. ("Am I on the vice beat today, lootenant?" "No,

O'Reilley, you are on the restaurant head-count detail. Shoot foist and count later.")

In many restaurants I've seen a sign, "Employees must wash their hands before leaving." It has always seemed to me that this somewhat disquieting thought would be more effectively conveyed by a quiet word from the restaurateur into the ear of a new employee. ("Luigi, this is what is called soap."). But in New York, at least, it must not only be done, it must be read to be done.

Or take a logical sign such as "No littering, smoking, or spitting." Fair enough, you say. So do I. But don't tell that to the New York City Transit Authority. The sign in the subway says: "New York City Health Code PROHIBITS on all New York Transportation facilities, LITTERING (or creating a nuisance or an unsanitary condition), SMOKING (or carrying an open flame, lighted match, cigarette, or pipe), SPITTING. Penalty, fine or imprisonment or both. Order of the New York Transportation Authority."

The elevator (lift) of the Portobello Hotel in London has a sign saying "Close both doors." In my imagination I can see how that might translate across the Atlantic:

> Dear Hotel Guest,
>
> For the comfort and convenience of other guests, you are respectfully requested when entering or leaving the elevator to ensure that both gates are fully closed, so as not to render the elevator inoperative, and thereby add to the inconvenience of those guests seeking to avail themselves of the facility. Thank you for your courtesy and cooperation. Have a nice day.
>
> The Management

I take it for granted that good writing style and grammatical error are incompatible. But what shall we say of those gray areas, where the grammatical rules are uncertain, or at any rate, have come unstuck recently? I am thinking of split infinitives and dangling prepositions. My own position is conservative. Split infinitives *always* should be avoided. Frequently it seems easier on the eye than any alternative. "He is a hard person to really know" sounds more mellifluous and less pompous than "He is a hard person really to know," or "He is a hard person to know really." The remedy here could be to change the word *really*. *Really* is a weaker word than, say, *completely* or *properly*. "He is a hard person to know completely" solves the problem, both grammatically and effectively.

A reader of novels is by definition an educated person. The act of reading makes him so. And the split infinitive irritates too many intelligent readers to warrant the intellectual laziness of permitting it. It nags like a caraway seed in the teeth.

It is the same with the dangling preposition. I know it is frequently a useful way to wind a sentence up. And we are told that it was something up with which Winston Churchill would not put. But as a matter of courtesy to the reader, if you can possibly find a way of avoiding dangling your prepositions, do so.

Earlier in this chapter I alluded to those thoughtless, perfunctory ways of expressing things that can make reading a bore. Plainly, the kind of expression I was talking about verges on the cliché. Yet I think there is a subtle distinction to be made, and that is why I have held off talking about clichés until now. A cliché is a perfunctory expression that is at once so threadbare of imagery and so utterly predictable (cliché) in context that it doesn't just slip by unnoticed (cliché); we actually do react to it, half in amusement, half in annoyance.

I am not absolutely opposed to clichés. On the contrary, I love them. The deliberate cliché is a delight to the reader because it *is* deliberate and a smashing literary weapon when used with care. P. G. Wodehouse raised the calculated cliché to the pinnacle of literature. I'll pull a couple of Wodehouses at random from my library: *How Right You Are, Jeeves*:

> I came away from the telephone on what practically amounted to leaden feet. Here, I was feeling, was a nice bit of box fruit. Bobbie

> Wickham with her tendency to stir things up and with each day to discover some new way of staggering civilization, would by herself have been bad enough. Add Aubrey Upjohn and the mixture became too rich. I don't know if Reginald (Kipper) Herring, when I rejoined him, noticed that my brow was sicklied o'er with the pale cast of thought, as I have heard Jeeves put it ... As had happened so often in the past, I was conscious of impending doom. Exactly what form this would take I was of course unable to say--it might be one thing or it might be another--but a voice seemed to whisper to me at some not distant date, Bertram Wooster was slated to get it in the gizzard.

And from *Hot Water*:

> Blair Eggleston was small and slim and, if you do not mind side-whiskers, and one of those little moustaches that look like soot, good-looking. He seemed nervous. There was not much of his moustache but he was tugging at what there was. He regarded Packy with a glassy eye.

And elsewhere, perhaps his most classic line, "Aunt Agatha entered the room like a galleon under sail."

Evelyn Waugh called Wodehouse "the Master." When someone suggested that this might be an exaggeration, the old curmudgeon replied that any author is entitled to be called "Master" if he can produce an average of three brilliant and unique similes to each page. (Waugh *was* exaggerating so don't get downhearted. One twentieth of that still can add up to a good book.)

In one chapter of my most recent book before this, *Best-seller:* A Nostalgic Celebration of the Less-Than-Great Novels You Have Always Been Afraid to Admit You Loved (New York: Wyndham, 1981), I piled cliché on cliché to achieve the ludicrous effect I was seeking. The chapter concerned dealt with *Forever Amber,* by Kathleen Winsor, and celebrated sex books in general. In the context I was fourteen years old and had suddenly turned the page to an unexpected sex scene in *My Son, My Son* by Howard Spring while my mother was making my tea at home in the north of England.

> For a lad wrestling with puberty this was pretty hot stuff! It should have been read alone in the bedroom. Not five feet away from me, my mother was cooking kippers for my tea.
>
> "What's the matter?" she said.
>
> "Nothing."
>
> "You're as red as a beetroot."
>
> My mother had warned me about nocturnal practices which might stunt my growth and, dread warning, give me dark rings under the eyes. She wanted me to get fresh air and make money. "Go outside and pick some pockets, yer little bleeder" she was accustomed to say, blowing the froth from her Guinness into the single eye of the family cur, and sipping her tea from the saucer, "And stop thinking dirty."
>
> She knew I was thinking about breasts, ladies' breasts and bare to boot. I was an exceedingly pale child.
>
> Mum looked over my shoulder. She was not wearing her glasses (nor her teeth for that matter), but she was no fool. She had once caught me trying in vain to find the dirty passages someone told me lurked in Thomas Hardy's *Two on a Tower.*
>
> "Another dirty book?" she asked. "You know what will happen? You'll grow up so small you'll have to be a jockey."
>
> *"Tiens!"*

This is an example of the cliché as a weapon. *Stunt your growth, hot stuff, red as a beetroot, dread warning, trying in vain.* Crumbs! If those had slithered in by accident instead of being laid as meticulously as a minefield, I would have given myself an *F.*

It is sometimes even possible to use a cliché effectively when no self-parody is intended. This is obviously true in dialogue, when you want to suggest that one of your characters is the sort of person who *would* normally use clichés without being aware of it. But there may be times when you yourself can use clichés in your own narrative prose. There is no rule for it, because the times in question are rare, and because you have to have an exceptionally good ear for prose rhythm to be able to get away with it. Clichés, tired and obvious though they may be, usually express the ideas, feelings, or images they signify with, if not power, considerable accuracy. And there may be times when that is just the level on which you want to convey something, neither freshly nor powerfully—most often in juxtaposition to another passage that is freighted almost too heavily with original metaphor. For example, consider this brief extract, taken virtually at random, from John Updike's *Bech Is Back* (New York: Knopf, 1982, page 105):

> Now Bech was installed in the mansion like a hermit crab tossed into a birdhouse. The place was much too big; he couldn't get used to the staircases and the volumes of air they arrogantly commandeered. . . . In the cellar you could see the oil tanks—two huge rust-brown things greasy to the touch. And here was the furnace, an old converted coal-burner in a crumbling overcoat of plastered asbestos, rumbling and muttering all through the night like a madman's brain. Bech had hardly ever visited a basement before; he had lived on the air, like mistletoe, like the hairy sloth, Manhattan sub-genus.

What an astonishing shower of similes and metaphors! Vivid, accurate, and just baroque enough to be consistently amusing. And Updike can go on like this for pages. So can Richard Condon. Yet, as no one knows better than Updike himself, there is a danger that a writer can go on too long like this. The reader becomes increasingly stunned by the sheer brilliance of his writing. His responses begin to flag. He needs something flatter and less demanding, a respite in which to catch his breath. That respite might consist of many things, and no doubt the least likely choice would be the deliberate use of a cliché or two. But the point is: It isn't a completely *impossible* choice—for a very skillful writer.

So, back to my most fundamental observation about creative writing: There are plenty of good rules to guide the writer, and none of them is absolute.

9

THE LAST STAGES

When you have the last draft of your novel done, the real hard work begins. Some writers insist that they do their best work in revision. But many other writers—and especially beginners—cannot bring themselves to recognize, let alone perform, the kind of surgery needed to make the novel work. In such cases, happy the writers who have good editors.

Since good revision and good line editing (or manuscript editing, so that it will not be confused with copy editing) are much the same, I shall treat them together under the general category of editing. This means that you have acquired the services of an experienced editor. And how do you do that? There are several possibilities. The most conventional way is for your editor to be provided by your publisher. And how do you find a publisher? Well...

It sometimes seems to me that some of my students are more concerned with learning how to find a good agent than they are with learning how to write. That is understandable. It is not easy for an unpublished author to attract a publisher's attention. But it is not as difficult as it is made out to be. Too many writers assume that they get rejection notices because their work hasn't been read by publisher's readers. The truth is that they probably get rejections because their stuff *has* been read. Publishers have no stake in turning down a good book. Even publishers who claim they don't accept unsolicited material will always take a peek at it to see it if has promise.

I have nothing against literary agents. They are wonderful people. I dedicated my last book to my own agent. Agents know which publishing houses are looking for what. They know the personal tastes of individual editors. They will read a manuscript and think, "This won't go at Knopf. But Jimmy at Doubleday loves this kind of book. Or maybe Crown." Agents always have a shrewd idea of how much to ask for in the way of advances and royalties. They are great negotiators. They are good to have on your side. But you can live without them.

If you elect to submit your manuscript without the help of an agent, here is a tip that I know to be helpful because I got it from the editor-in-chief of a major publishing house. Always submit your manuscript to an individual editor and make sure that that editor is *not* the editor-in-chief. The editor-in-chief is always overworked, overwhelmed. He will pass the manuscript, unread, to an assistant for prescreening. It will wind up not at the top of the heap of manuscripts, but with the most junior editorial trainee who, in the charming jargon of publishing, is in charge of the "slush pile."

Thus, if you want your manuscript read by someone senior, do not simply send it to the publisher or to the fiction editor or to the editor-in-chief. Instead, go to the library and get hold of the current edition of *Literary Market Place*, the annual publication put out by R. R. Bowker Company that lists the names, titles, addressses, and telephone numbers of virtually everyone in the publishing business. Choose at random the name of a senior editor in the house of your choice and send him or her your manuscript. The fit may not be ideal; you could be dealing with someone temperamentally unsuited to your kind of writing. But you will be dealing not with an overworked tyro, but with an experienced professional who may at least have the wit to pass your submission—if it warrants it—to the right colleague. To get even that far in one of today's busy publishing houses is, as Henri IV said of being a Breton duke, no small beer.

I am getting ahead of myself. Let's go back to the moment when you realize that you are ready to submit. Your novel is completed and needs only to be typed and mailed. We now touch on the important subject of presentation.

Let us assume that it is Friday evening and the lights are going out in the publishers' offices in New York. A publisher has two manuscripts on her desk, and she is deciding which one to take for weekend reading "out on the island" (for some reason publishers all seem to spend their weekends on the island, at the shore, or in the Hamptons). One manuscript is typed and presented in a professional way. The other is a typographical shambles. You do not have to think very hard to decide which one she will take.

I always type every page of my final draft myself. It sounds time-consuming and it is, but somehow I always find something that can be improved, polished, honed—no matter how many times I have rewritten and revised.

The typewriter should have a keyboard in pica type, not the smaller elite type sometimes used by secretaries. There are several reasons for this. Pica is easier to read, especially when many thousands of words are involved. It is also an easier type for the author to work with. An average manuscript page in pica type will amount to about 250 words. A page of elite will be closer to 300 words. So each page you revise will mean 20 percent more physical labor for you, and I can tell you from painful experience on one elite typewriter that at the end of a hard day's work, it feels like much more!

I keep half a dozen typewriters. Two electric typewriters, one for town and one for country. A medium-sized typewriter waits for me in London, and an ultra-lightweight I keep in a corner for air travel. There are two more kept in reserve in case one or another breaks down. All have identical pica type so that the publisher will be given the impression of professional continuity: that the manuscript has come off one typewriter. To heighten this comfortable impression I give my typewriter ribbons a shorter life than is necessary and discard them as soon as they begin to fade even slightly. It is amazing how many professional writers neglect this small but important point. A friend of mine who has sold about three novels and several nonfiction books wrote me recently, bleating that his manuscripts were being returned to him. I could easily see why. I could hardly read his letter because his ribbon was so faint.

Publishers like wide left-hand margins to allow them space for their pencil marks. My left-hand margins are always two inches deep. Publishers need to breathe the air of white paper. At the bottom of the page I try to leave another two inches of white space, for my own convenience as well as the publisher's. I might decide upon rereading that the page needs a rewrite that will add a couple of lines.

Clean type is also important. Larry Freundlich of Wyndham Books, who published my book *Bestseller*, told me he is physically repelled by a manuscript in which the o, e, and a emerge as ●, e, and a.

The manuscript does not have to be perfect. Publishers do not care much for xxx's and mmnmnmnm's, but as long as the story holds their interest they will put up with it. I have found that to erase with a thick black marker and a ruler effectively wipes the erasure out of a publisher's and editor's consciousness. Perhaps it conveys an impression of neatness, which xxxxxxx does not.

The manuscript should probably be the conventional black type on white paper, though I have read a manuscript typed in sepia-brown that was very restful to the eye.

One reason why a publisher will tolerate modest imperfections in a manuscript is that she worries about writers. A first novel arriving unsolicited on her desk obviously typed by a professional typist may cause her to react: "God! This must have cost the author four hundred dollars, and here I am sending it back with four hundred dollars on my conscience!"

The psychological result could be inhibition, a reluctance

to touch the beautiful bundle with a rude pencil; an inhibition that intensifies if the manuscript arrives bound. A fiction manuscript is not a doctoral thesis that has to be bound and typed to perfection. There is always the fear lurking in the publisher's mind that he or she can be wrong, and any notes made on a bound perfect manuscript will compromise the author's chances of selling it elsewhere. Better be safe. Send it back. For that reason a publisher is always thankful to receive a loose manuscript in a cardboard box, the kind that contains typing paper.

I was surprised to be told by several students that publishers will draw up a contract for a novel on the basis of some specimen chapters and a summary of what is to come. They had read it somewhere in some specialist magazines. This is not my experience or that of publishers to whom I have spoken on the subject. It is certainly not the practice with fiction, unless one's work is well known and admired by the publisher. Take it for granted that your novel should be completed before it is submitted.

Let us say that you have submitted your complete manuscript and that it has been accepted. Now begins one of the most painful and illuminating phases of the entire writing process: the phase in which for the first time you relinquish your cherished creation into the hands of another person—probably a stranger—so that he or she can edit it.

For the sake of simplicity, I have so far been assuming that that first other person will be a member of your publisher's editorial staff, but in reality it might be your agent or your creative writing teacher. Whoever it is, the result is bound to be something of a shock to your ego. And if you permit it to be too much of a shock, if you treat each criticism as an affront rather than as a potentially valuable gift, you are probably doomed.

You may recall my telling you that the first person to look at the results of my first attempt at writing fiction was a wonderfully accomplished editor, Knox Burger. I still have the preliminary comments he sent me. Here is a sampling:

> Your opening is weak. However, if you turn to page 73, second paragraph, I think you will agree that it would make a gripping

start, especially if you follow it with a flashback to the sequence which begins on page 15 in the manuscript.

Dorothy and Priscilla are too similar in character. I think they could be telescoped into one.

P. 81. I think the sex here could be implied rather than be made explicit.

Tom is a stick throughout and slows down the action whenever you bring him in. Either cut him out altogether, or think of ways you can make him more interesting.

p. 181. The fight scene is GREAT!!!!!!

And so on for page after page. I followed the same technique with my students when I was a professor of creative writing.

You do not have to take all professional criticism as gospel, because professionals can be wrong too. But on the other hand, arrogance by the author has killed many a potential novel. Some years ago, a friend whom I will call Bill showed me the manuscript of his first novel. Bill was a professional magazine writer, a former newspaper reporter, and a foreign correspondent. He wrote one of those rare novels in which the theme is riveting even in a brief description. It is about a lovable slob of a newspaper reporter called Joe. He loves his mother and his girl friend. He helps old ladies cross the road, repairs his neighbors' television set, drinks beer from the can, and is an easy touch for his pals. But he is overweight, a messy eater, and seems to own only one suit. His girl friend issues an ultimatum: smarten up or else. Joe goes on a crash diet, has his suits made to measure, visits elegant hairdressers, and studies wine. At each stage of his education he becomes less lovable, meaner, and ends up as the editor of the paper and detested by everybody.

It was a variation on the old theme of whether it is better to be an old man's queen or a young man's slave. I enthusiastically promoted the book to a publisher, warning him also that it needed a lot of work, and the publisher drew up a contract. Out of friendship for Bill I went over the manuscript the way Knox Burger had gone over mine, spelling out my views line by line. I telephoned Bill to say that I had finished. He stopped by to pick up the manuscript—but left the notes behind, unread. "Hello," I said to myself, warning bells jingling in my ears.

Another fine original writer and a lawyer, whom I will call Tom, was one of my potentially most exciting students. I put him onto a publisher I felt sure would love his manuscript, but *warned* him, "Tom, you are an arguer, in love with your own words. If the publisher likes the book and suggests changes, listen. Don't argue, explain, or theorize. If you do, the publisher will say to himself, 'Oh, oh! He'll criticize the copy editing, complain of slow progress, hit the roof over the jacket, be on the telephone all the time. Not worth the trouble. Pity. It's a good book, but no thanks.'"

It is commonplace among editors to say that the way a writer responds to editing is a sure index of how professional he is. It is not the best-selling authors (some of whom need lots of help) who give their editors the most trouble; it is the too sensitive beginners. Which may be one reason why many editors think twice before taking on first novels.

What is it that makes a good editor's intervention so valuable? How can an editor pretend to know more about how a particular novel should be written than the person who created it? The fact is that an editor may often bring to a manuscript only one thing that its author cannot. *Objectivity.*

The author will have been totally immersed in his novel for months or even years. He will have rewritten scenes countless times, changed characters, restructured the plot, fiddled endlessly with passages of dialogue. He will have lavished so much attention on stylistic details and bits of narrative machinery that he will—almost inevitably—have lost his ability to see how the whole book works on first reading. It is the old problem of the forest and the trees.

But the editor *is* a first-time reader. And more than that, he is a reader who, unlike most of us, is trained not just to stop at saying vaguely "I kind of lost interest toward the end," or "The Priscilla character never grabbed me, somehow." Instead, the editor tries to use all his professional skills both to identify, as explicitly as possible, the weaknesses and to propose what to do about them.

Of course, the more time an editor spends with a manuscript, the more he will distance himself from his first impressions and the more his own objectivity will erode. That is why wise authors—and editors—always should pay careful attention to the editor's first impressions.

Nor should you scorn an editor's suggestions because they seem painful to your pride, difficult to accomplish, or simply something that you have never even considered. A good remedy can work magic. I will give you two examples.

My novel *The Fourth Horseman* is about a gang of English and Irish renegades who descend on Hollywood Park racetrack and steal not only the money from the money room but every purse, pocketbook, and wallet from the 35,000 spectators. For purposes of the plot, the central character Brownlow, a disgraced SAS officer, needs a financial genius. He knows just the man, Kolev, a defector from the Soviet Union living in a sleazy district of Paris:

> He pressed the bell to Kolev's flat. He had expected the natural caution from a man with so many enemies in the Soviet Union and so many solicitors of aid among impoverished Russians in the west. He expected double-locks, chains, a barking dog, or at least a muttered "Who's there?" from the other side of the door. Instead it was flung open with a crash that snowed plaster from the walls, by a man naked except for a pair of baggy drawers. Everything about him seemed to wave, wriggle and gibber. He capered first on one leg and then the other. The arms gesticulated at a rate that reminded Brownlow of a four-armed Indian dancing God. Unkempt hair flew about wild, red-rimmed eyes. The man was a giant, at least six feet four inches in height. But most disconcert-

ing of all was a Webley automatic held aloft in his right hand, enabling Brownlow to note that it was fully loaded.

"Are you José André Lacour, you pig?" the apparition yelled. "Or Prakhorenko?"

"Neither."

"Sure you're not Prakhorenko? You look like Prakhorenko!"

Brownlow considered his past confrontations with armed adversaries. He coped. He soothed. Gently he led Kolev into the flat and took the gun from his hand.... Kolev flung his tangled dust-smelling hair on Brownlow's shoulders, overwhelmed him with his size, almost knocking him to the rug. Kolev sobbed. "Why do the Americans debilitate themselves to keep the Soviet Union afloat? Why don't they do the Russians a favor and let the system rot of its own putrescence?" Brownlow freed himself, took his silk handkerchief from his breast pocket and wiped away Kolev's tears. He sat the professor on a creaking settee, found a corkscrew to open the vodka bottle and two clean glasses. When Kolev's emotions subsided, Brownlow sat facing him and addressed him in carefully worded French.

"First of all, Joseph Alexandrovitch, I have a financial proposition which will appeal to you. But before I make it, I want to ask you, who is the most evil man in the world?"

"My father," said Kolev smiling. "Papa."

"Wrong."

"You never met the bugger. During the Stalin purges of the 1930's, Papa would take out the family album and ink out the face of each former comrade as he was executed. He told me and my beloved sister, Rosa, 'When you cut down the forests, the chips must fly. My time will come.' The old sod kept an attaché case containing toiletries and change of underwear, waiting for the knock on the door in the small hours..."

Anyone who read *The Fourth Horseman* may be excused a puzzled frown. "Out!" said my editor, James Wade, his Irish eyes unsmiling as he ran a pencil through the whole scene (which continues for several more pages). Furious arguments ensued. "Kolev is the most colorful character in the whole book," I yelled.

"I don't disagree," said Wade, "and I am sure he will be the most colorful character in your next book. But he slows down the narrative. He does not fit in with the other characters. Besides, you have already introduced the girl to whom you attribute an exceptionally high IQ. Make her the financial genius the gang needs. . . ."

Wade was right. But I have not thrown Kolev away. I have filed him, as James Wade knew I would, for my next novel. The moral is that almost no author can reliably cut his own novel. There are too many scenes and characters that he loves for the wrong reasons. The author who is asked to cut 100 pages from his novel will certainly cut the wrong 100. It is one of the facts of novel writing.

Another example, less painful because I wasn't on the receiving end: The authoress, Linda Wells asked me to read her excellent novel about the War of Independence, *Patriot's Lady*, before mailing it to her publisher. I saw that here and there, through overenthusiasm, she had fallen into the error of too much direct narrative. A few suggestions on my part, I think, corrected her faults and emphasized a basic tenet of fiction writing: almost every sentence should provide a counterpoint to the previous sentence. Here is a page of Linda Wells's manuscript, with the faults underlined.

> They galloped down the road at a dead run. Sarah dared to think they were safe. At the fork leading to the Jamestown road, she heard horses. Were they behind her? She couldn't tell. No, they were coming from Greensward.
>
> Jackson pulled on his rein, the horses rearing to a halt. "They've found us out. We must bluff or make a run for it."
>
> "Run for it!" shouted Sarah.
>
> Jackson jerked the reins and turned the horses down the road which led away from Williamsburg and toward Jamestown. "If we escape, we can go around and take an old path I remember."
>
> Sarah could only nod. She bumped up and down in the saddle. Unable to keep her seat with the stirrup too long for her legs, she flew into the air with every jolt. She was too frightened to feel pain.

The horsemen were gaining on them. She heard Stuart call her name. "Sarah! Stop!" She saw the flash of powder. A shot was fired. She heard the crack seconds later. They fired another shot. She heard Stuart cursing the man with the gun. In the black void through which they hurtled, *she heard* a horse scream in pain.

The page had to be edited to eliminate the constant repetition of "she heard," "she bumped," "she flew," "she saw," "she was," and so on. By use of the counterpoint to each succeeding sentence, the task was easy and made for better narrative.

They galloped down the road at a dead run. Sarah dared to think she was safe. At the fork leading to the Jamestown road, she heard horses. Were they coming behind her? (Original: she couldn't tell.) No, they were coming from Greensward.

Jackson pulled on his rein, the horse rearing to a halt. "They've found us out. We must bluff or make a run for it."

"Run for it!" shouted Sarah.

Jackson jerked the reins and turned the horses down the road which led away from Williamsburg and toward Jamestown. "If we escape, we can go around and take an old path I remember."

Sarah could only nod. (Original: she bumped.) Every jolt of the horse sent her flying into the air (Original: she flew), her feet losing stirrups that were too long for her legs, but her fear (Original: she was too frightened) obliterated her pain.

The horsemen were gaining on them. Stuart called her name. (Original: She heard Stuart call her name.) "Sarah! Stop!" Powder flashed in the darkness. (Original: she saw a flash.) The crack of the shot was heard seconds later. (Original: she heard the crack.) They fired another shot. She heard (as in original) Stuart curse (instead of "cursing" in original) the man with the gun. In the black void through which they hurtled, a horse screamed in pain. (Original: she heard a horse scream.)

These examples suggest the two main ways in which the manuscript editor can help the author. In the first example, Jim Wade's advice about deleting Kolev—like Knox Burger's earlier advice about Dorothy and Priscilla, Tom, and where the novel should begin—had to do with large structural matters. This is where the editor's fresh vision is likely to be most useful, for it is about the big picture that the writer's judgment may be most uncertain.

The second example, my advice to Linda Wells, was of a different order, more narrowly focused on technique. Not all editors are sufficiently good writers themselves to be able to give this kind of advice—which doesn't mean that they don't try. When an editor gives you detailed technical advice on your writing style, listen but be cautious. He may be right; he may be right for someone else but not for you; or he may be dead wrong.

Once past the trauma—or maybe eye-opening pleasure—of manuscript editing, you will move on to the vital phase of copy editing. One day your publisher will send your manuscript back to you, its pages covered with myriad little varicolored pencilings—all apparently designed to prove to you that you know nothing of spelling, punctuation, or grammar, and that you are not even capable of remembering between page 7 and 243 the correct middle initial of your heroine's name. There is seldom much you can do with a copy-edited manuscript except to answer the copy editor's queries, but you should go over it carefully, all the same. Copy editors have been known to get misguided bees in their bonnets, such as scrupulously correcting in dialogue grammatical errors that the author had deliberately inserted to show his character's lack of education.

In one of my novels I have an Irish terrorist whom I called Erroll Flynn. My alert copy editor commented that I has misspelled the movie star's name. She was right, and I had not noticed. So rather than correct the misspelling on page after page, I turned it to a certain small advantage and inserted, "Poor Mrs. Flynn even misspelled the name of her own child, and he grew up to be extremely ugly and never forgave her."

Other phases will follow—proofreading, obtaining permissions for quoted matter, answering publicity questionnaires, approving jacket copy, and so on—each more remote than the last from the true creative writing process, and all contained within the seemingly endless waiting period between finished manuscript and printed book.

There is much to be said about the many subtle and unexpected pressures that beset an author on his way to, and following, publication, but they lie beyond the scope of what this book is meant to be about: the craft of fiction writing. So I shall simply repeat a bit of advice I gave you earlier: the minute you finish your first novel, begin working on the second. If you can understand why I say this, so much the better. If not, trust me.

And now, to my surprise, I find that I have finished. I have told you most of the things I set out to tell you, and yet I know that I have barely scratched the surface of the huge, mysterious subject of imaginative writing. I know, too, that I haven't even been a very good exemplar. You will have spotted in this book all too many of the flaws I solemnly warn my students against (such as ending a sentence with a preposition like against).

At the end of one of my classes I walked down the corridor behind two of my students who did not know I was there. I shall even name the hussies. Cindy Mounts and Virginia Hutchins. I heard one say to the other, "He's been quoting his own works again, doing everything he tells us not to do, dangling his prepositions, using *as* in the middle of a sentence, splitting infinitives, the works. . . ."

The other replied, "Do what the man says, not what he does."

Now that Cindy and Virginia are both published authors, I can only presume that they are committing the same "errors" on their own. And, because they are both such good writers, I have no doubt that they will be doing so in the most deliberate, appropriate, and effective way imaginable.

GEOFFREY BOCCA

was the prolific and successful author of eleven novels, seven biographies, four travel books, three histories, and one volume of literary criticism. As Author in Residence and teacher of creative writing, he was associated with several American universities, most recently with Pennsylvania State University. Mr. Bocca died suddenly in London on July 8, 1983, while correcting the galleys of this, his last, book.

INDEX